# The Musical World of Walt Disney

Library of Congress Cataloging-in-Publication Data

Tietyen, David
    The musical world of Walt Disney/David Tietyen;
preface by Robert B. and Richard M. Sherman.

        p.   cm.
Includes index.
ISBN 0-88188-476-6
1. Motion Pictures and music.   2. Disney, Walt;
1901-1966.
I. Title.
ML2075.T56 1990
782.8′5′0973--dc19                    88-39879

# The Musical World of

David Tietyen

Preface by
Richard M. and
Robert B. Sherman

**Hal Leonard Publishing Corporation**

# ACKNOWLEDGMENTS

Thanks to Bourne Co., Walt Disney Music Company, and Wonderland Music Company, Inc. for permission to reproduce lyrics from the following songs:

**Baby Mine**
Words by Ned Washington. Music by Frank Churchill. Copyright © 1941 by Bourne Co. Copyright renewed. All rights reserved. Used by permission.

**The Ballad of Davy Crockett**
Words by Tom Blackburn. Music by George Bruns. Copyright © 1954 by Wonderland Music Company, Inc. Copyright renewed. International copyright secured. All rights reserved. Used by permission.

**Chim Chim Cher-ee**
Words and Music by Richard M. Sherman and Robert B. Sherman. Copyright © 1963 by Wonderland Music Company, Inc. International copyright secured. All rights reserved. Used by permission.

**A Dream Is a Wish Your Heart Makes**
Words and Music by Mack David, Al Hoffman and Jerry Livingston. Copyright © 1948 by Walt Disney Music Company. Copyright renewed. International copyright secured. All rights reserved. Used by permission.

**Feed the Birds**
Words and Music by Richard M. Sherman and Robert B. Sherman. Copyright © 1963 by Wonderland Music Company, Inc. International copyright secured. All rights reserved. Used by permission.

**Fortuosity**
Words and Music by Richard M. Sherman and Robert B. Sherman. Copyright © 1966 by Wonderland Music Company, Inc. International copyright secured. All rights reserved. Used by permission.

**Heigh-Ho (The Dwarfs' Marching Song)**
Words by Larry Morey. Music by Frank Churchill. Copyright © 1938 by Bourne Co. Copyright renewed. All rights reserved. Used by permission.

**I'm Late**
Words by Bob Hilliard. Music by Sammy Fain. Copyright © 1949 by Walt Disney Music Company. Copyright renewed. International copyright secured. All rights reserved. Used by permission.

**I'm Wishing**
Words by Larry Morey. Music by Frank Churchill. Copyright © 1937 by Bourne Co. Copyright renewed. All rights reserved. Used by permission.

**I've Got No Strings**
Words by Ned Washington. Music by Leigh Harline. Copyright © 1940 by Bourne Co. Copyright renewed. All rights reserved. Used by permission.

**It's a Small World**
Words and Music by Richard M. Sherman and Robert B. Sherman. Copyright © 1963 by Wonderland Music Company, Inc. International copyright secured. All rights reserved. Used by permission.

**Minnie's Yoo-Hoo**
Words by Walt Disney and Carl Stalling. Music by Carl Stalling. Copyright © 1930 by Walt Disney Music Company. Copyright renewed. International copyright secured. All rights reserved. Used by permission.

**Pink Elephants on Parade**
Words by Ned Washington. Music by Oliver Wallace. Copyright © 1940 by Bourne Co. Copyright renewed. All rights reserved. Used by permission.

**Say It with a Slap**
Words and Music by Eliot Daniel. Copyright © 1945 by Walt Disney Music Company. International copyright secured. All rights reserved. Used by permission.

**When I See an Elephant Fly**
Words by Ned Washington. Music by Oliver Wallace. Copyright © 1940 by Bourne Co. Copyright renewed. All rights reserved. Used by permission.

**When You Wish upon a Star**
Words by Ned Washington. Music by Leigh Harline. Copyright © 1940 by Bourne Co. Copyright renewed. All rights reserved. Used by permission.

**Whistle While You Work**
Words by Larry Morey. Music by Frank Churchill. Copyright © 1937 by Bourne Co. Copyright renewed. All rights reserved. Used by permission.

**Who's Afraid of the Big Bad Wolf**
Words by Frank Churchill and Ann Ronell. Music by Frank Churchill. Copyright © 1933 by Bourne Co. Copyright renewed. All rights reserved. Used by permission.

**Zip-A-Dee-Doo-Dah**
Words by Ray Gilbert. Music by Allie Wrubel. Copyright © 1945 by Walt Disney Music Company. Copyright renewed. International copyright secured. All rights reserved. Used by permission.

**Special thanks to:**

All of the Disney songwriters, for their contribution of the words and music that have warmed the hearts of millions throughout the world;

Richard M. and Robert B. Sherman, for graciously agreeing to write the Preface;

David R. Smith, for his generous assistance in compiling the historical information for this book;

And most importantly, to Walt Disney—whose vision helped us all to believe that our dreams really can come true.

# CONTENTS

# PREFACE

The talented composers, lyricists, and musicians referred to in this definitive volume were all touched by the magic of a very special man. As David Tietyen points out, Walt Disney didn't compose a note or orchestrate a single measure, but his sure sense of what was musically correct for his projects was always present. The internationally loved songs and scores that flowed from his films, television productions, and theme park attractions for over fifty years attest to this.

For almost a decade, starting in 1960, we wrote songs in a modern office building situated at the corner of Mickey Avenue and Dopey Drive in Burbank, California. This whimsical address does not appear on any street map, but it does exist at the Walt Disney Studios. There, under the aegis of a true entertainment genius, we became part of the creative team he hand-picked, nurtured, guided, chided and, most of all, inspired.

Walt often referred to himself as a "busy bee buzzing from flower to flower pollinating his garden." We were blessed with a generous portion of that "Disney pollen." Walt's up-beat, positive philosophy of life was contagious. His love of nature and compassion for all living things was constantly expressed in the stories, music, and lyrics of his productions. Though many years have passed since we were Walt Disney's staff songwriters, questions he so often asked us still come to mind whenever we start a new song: "Is this necessary to the story?"; "Will people care about the characters?," "What's happening on the screen during the song?," "What's fresh about it?," "What's different about it?," and always, "Is it in good taste?"

There was an excitement in the air when Walt was in a story meeting. He brought everyone to the peak of his creativity. Working on his staff brought us many exhilarating moments, but we both agree that the most special moments happened after we would demonstrate a new song for him. he would go into deep concentration and then, if he liked it, he'd simply say, "That'll work." What a sense of triumph we got from those words and all they implied. We know so many of our predecessors must have felt that same thrill. We'll remember that feeling as long as we live.

Richard M. Sherman
Robert B. Sherman
Beverly Hills, California
March 13, 1989

*"I do not make films primarily for children.
I make them for the child in all of us, whether
we be six or sixty. Call the child innocence.
The worst of us is not without innocence."*

*Walt Disney*

# CHAPTER ONE

For generations, the music of Walt Disney has enthralled us as much as his films. From "Who's Afraid of the Big Bad Wolf?" to "Zip-A-Dee-Doo-Dah," the music and songs have become as much a part of our culture as Mickey Mouse and Donald Duck.

Walt Disney was not a musician, he was a cartoonist. In fact, from all reports, he had no formal music education. Yet, the music and songs that flowed from his studio have become a part of our American heritage. These are songs that evoke fond childhood memories— memories of being caught up in the magical fantasies created by Disney. His music was cheerful, carrying a message of hope; appealing to all generations with a universal theme that life has much to offer. Disney's films were not children's films but they touched the child in all of us. As one Disney songwriter commented, "His most successful films had heart. There was always something in them that would reach out and touch one of our human emotions. This is what Walt added to each film he was personally involved with."

Walt Disney's lack of formal musical training did not deter him from being involved with the music in his films. Because he recognized the tremendous impact music added to a film, he devoted as much attention to the music as he did to every other aspect of film production. "There's a terrific power to music," he told his staff of animators and directors. "You can run these pictures and they'd be dragging and boring, but the minute you put music behind them, they have life and vitality they don't get in any other way." Over the years, Disney's films have demonstrated his inherent feeling for music—that special ability to recognize what style and type of music best fits a scene—and his unerring ear for the magical sounds that would enhance his pictures.

With the advent of sound in motion pictures, Disney recognized how important music could be to a film, especially an animated film or cartoon. He suggested to his directors, "I think a good study of music would be indispensable to the animators—a realization on their part of how primitive music is, how natural it is for people to want to go to music—a study of the rhythm, the dance—the various rhythms that enter into our lives every day."

Two of his animators, Frank Thomas and Ollie Johnston, in their book *Disney Animation*, note, "Music is undoubtedly the most important addition that will be made to the picture. It can do more to bring a production to life, to give it integrity, style, emphasis, meaning and unity, than any other single ingredient. With the surge of a full orchestra, there will be bigness and majesty and soaring spirits; with a nervous, fluttering melody line on a single instrument, or pulsating drumbeats, there will be agitation, apprehension, suspicion. Music can build tension in commonplace scenes or ease it in ones that have become visually too frightening."

Disney's appreciation for the role of music in film was so total that he built entire animated films on music. One of his achievements was *Fantasia*, in which he challenged and inspired his animators to create visual images that would bring classical music to life. As his first music director, Carl Stalling, noted, "That was his genius, I think, inspiring the people who worked for him to come up with new ideas."

Under Walt Disney's direction, his staff of composers and songwriters explored and charted new directions for music. They developed new techniques and approaches that resulted in the perfect blending of film and music. Disney was an innovator and technical pioneer. Original methods his studio developed for synchronizing music and action are still used today throughout the film industry. Even the cartoon director at rival Warner Brothers, Chuck Jones, acknowledged, "Practically every tool we use today was originated at the Disney studio—not necessarily by Walt, but his men couldn't have originated them unless he encouraged them to exist."

At the Disney studio, film and music were a cohesive unit. As the art of animation and films evolved, so did the sophistication and use of music. But Disney films did not just evolve, they took quantum leaps, reaching beyond the state of the art to take films and music to new plateaus.

There are distinct stages to this evolution of film and music. In the early Mickey Mouse cartoons music was a novelty, as was sound, and Disney used it for its comedy value. The term "mickey mousing," which is still used today, refers to the close synchronization of music with cartoon action.

Disney recognized that music could play a much larger role in animated films. He then launched an experimental cartoon series, *Silly Symphonies*, that used music as the focal point. With these not-so-silly musical productions, his animators and staff were able to develop and refine techniques that later would be used so skillfully in his feature-length animated films. The success of this experiment is best described in the words of the great American composer Jerome Kern, who said, "Cartoonist Walt Disney has made the twentieth century's only important contribution to music. Disney has made use of music as language. In the synchronization of humorous episodes with humorous music, he has unquestionably given us the outstanding contribution of our time. In fact, I would go so far as to say it is the only real contribution."

In the next stage of evolution, Disney went beyond the short cartoon to produce feature-length animated films. His first, *Snow White and the Seven Dwarfs*, was a carefully crafted musical in an animated setting. The evolution and development of the animated feature has continued at the Disney studio for more than fifty years since *Snow White* was put into production.

A brief stage of music development occurred following World War II and involved the exploitation of music in a series of entertaining animated films featuring short segments with well-known entertainers such as Dinah Shore and Nelson Eddy. This experience was put to good use in later animated features such as *Lady and the Tramp*, which featured Peggy Lee.

The final stage of evolution was during the Sixties when Disney produced a number of musicals. The most ambitious, and most successful, was *Mary Poppins*, which is a showcase of the best of Disney in animation, live action, and songs.

# It Started with a Mouse

Walter Elias Disney, who preferred to be called simply "Walt," had his roots in midwestern America. He was born in 1901 in Chicago, but lived much of his young life in Marceline and Kansas City, Missouri. His childhood experiences were to play an important part in later years, and films such as *Snow White*, *Peter Pan*, *Cinderella*, and *Alice in Wonderland* can be traced to his memories as a young boy.

After serving as a Red Cross ambulance driver in France at the end of World War I, the seventeen-year-old Disney returned to Kansas City and began working as a commercial artist. During this period he met Ub Iwerks, who later became Disney's first animator, and the two eventually began making their own cartoons. It was also during this period that Walt became acquainted with Carl Stalling, a theater organist who later became the studio's first music director.

Stalling, in an interview in *Funnyworld*, recalled, "... I first met Walt Disney in the early Twenties. He used to come to the Isis Theater where I played the organ and had my own orchestra.... Walt was making short commercials at the time, and he'd have us run them for him.... Walt left for Hollywood shortly after that time and I didn't see him again until 1928. I started writing him when sound pictures came in, and in our correspondence back and forth, we just agreed that there would be a position for a musical director at his studio."

Disney's cartoon efforts were not an immediate success in Kansas City, and he and his older brother, Roy, moved separately to Los Angeles in search of opportunity. It was there that the Disney Brothers Studio was launched when, ironically, Walt received word that a New York film distributor was interested in a cartoon Walt had developed in Kansas City. This first Disney cartoon series, the *Alice Comedies*, was a combination of live action and limited animation. In 1927, Disney began a new cartoon series called

*Oswald The Lucky Rabbit*, and the series proved so successful that the New York distributor decided to take it over. Faced with the choice of continuing to work on *Oswald* at a low salary and without control, Walt took a risk and opted for artistic freedom. *Oswald* later ended up at Universal with Walter Lantz doing the animation.

According to Disney legend, it was while on his way back from the disastrous meeting with his New York distributor that Walt created Mickey Mouse (the character was almost named Mortimer).

Just as Mickey Mouse launched Walt Disney on the road to fame, Mickey played a major role in bringing music to Disney films. Following his return to Hollywood, Walt and his fledging studio staff began to work furiously on producing Mickey Mouse cartoons. Unfortunately, the first two cartoons, *Plane Crazy* and *Gallopin' Gaucho*, were not well-received by the distributors, and Disney was unable to sell them. Several months before these first Mickey Mouse cartoons were finished, Warner Brothers released *The Jazz Singer*, and Walt paid careful attention to the commercial success that the film was experiencing. Although mainstream Hollywood producers were cautious about "talking" pictures, Walt could foresee that the days of the silent film were numbered, and he recognized the potential that sound could hold for a film's success, particularly when applied to cartoons. Rather than continue trying to sell the two Mickey cartoons, he concentrated on adding sound to the third cartoon that was in production at the time, *Steamboat Willie*.

Disney's approach to sound was as painstakingly precise as his approach to animation. He did not just want to add sound, as was being done in some cartoons, he wanted to *synchronize* the sound with the action. But of course animated drawings don't make any sound, so a method of synchronizing sound with the movements of animated characters had to be developed.

Wilfred Jackson, a young animator who went on to become a leading director at the Disney studio, is credited with devising a system for synchronization that is still being used nearly sixty years later. Although he was not a professional musician, Jackson did have some early music training which he put

Walt Disney, with brother Roy (right), 1932.

*Opposite:* Early photo of Walt, circa 1919-1920.

to use in solving the problem. He knew that film ran through a projector at 90 feet per minute, or 24 frames per second. Using a metronome, he could coordinate the beat of the music with the film. For example, with the metronome set at 60, there would be one beat every second, or every 24 frames. When the metronome was set at 120, there was one beat every 12 frames.

In an interview published in *Funnyworld*, Jackson recalled the experience with *Steamboat Willie*: "I played the harmonica so that Walt could tell the tempo that he wanted for 'Steamboat Bill' and 'Turkey in the Straw'(two tunes used for the picture). I would set the metronome and play 'Steamboat Bill' or 'Turkey' or whatever, and when Walt heard what sounded good for the tune and his action both, then he knew that was the beat he wanted. Walt knew how fast the film went, and I knew about the metronome. Putting the two together make it possible to pre-time music to animation when the music would be recorded later, just by simple mathematics.

"Walt made up the exposure sheet for 'Willie.' What I worked out was a bar sheet, or dope sheet, to indicate measures of music. It wasn't like a score because it didn't have five bar lines. It had a little square for each beat in each measure, and it had an indication of the tempo; it was in twelve frames, or sixteen frames, or whatever, to the beat. Within that square, the key action and the scene number was indicated, so that the bar sheet showed that each scene began so many frames before a certain measure. That way, we were able to synchronize the scenes, which were shot separately, of course. Each individual scene would be shot from the exposure sheet, but from the bar sheet, you could tell how to lay the scene in against the music track, once you found out where the first beat of the measure was. My contributions to sound cartoons were that I knew what a metronome was, and I worked out what was first called a dope sheet and later a bar sheet."

Jackson used this technique to "score" *Steamboat Willie* complete with music, dialogue and sound effects. In the short cartoon, a goat eats the sheet music for "Turkey in the Straw," at which point Mickey begins cranking its tail like an old-fashioned hurdy-gurdy and the music plays, with the notes

*Steamboat Willie* — the first Disney cartoon in which sound was synchronized with the action.

streaming from the goat's mouth. In other scenes, more barnyard animals add their musical accompaniment, including a cow's teeth being played as a xylophone.

Despite the fact that Walt now had a technique that enabled him to match sound with his film's action, he met resistance from the major recording studios in New York. They weren't interested in having a "cartoonist" tell them how to record a soundtrack. Finally Walt found an independent, or *outlaw*, studio headed by Pat Powers that seemed willing to let him have his way.

Powers found a conductor, Carl Edouarde, who was the orchestra director at New York's Strand Theatre. To help the conductor, Walt drew marks on the film to indicate each musical beat. These would appear as white flashes on the screen and provided the conductor with a visual metronome coordinated to the film. Unfortunately, Edouarde ignored the flashes and conducted the orchestra by trying to follow the action, a technique he used when accompanying silent films at the theater. To finance another recording session, Walt had to wire his brother Roy for money—a position that Roy found himself in many times during the early days at the studio. At the next recording session, Edouarde followed the flashes and Walt had a successful soundtrack.

*Steamboat Willie* premiered at New York's Colony Theater on November 18, 1928. Mickey Mouse's debut was an instant success, and within weeks, the film was playing at the prestigious Roxy Theater.

William Paul, in the article "Art, Music, Nature and Walt Disney" appearing in the English publication *Movie*, writes, "...*Steamboat Willie* distinguishes itself from earlier attempts at sound cartoons by being organized around its soundtrack.... The result is a barnyard surrealism with commonplace sights and sounds comically recast, transforming the details of farm life into an exotic *tour de force*."

On his way to New York for the recording session, Walt had stopped in Kansas City and left the two earlier as-yet-unreleased Mickey cartoons with Stalling to score. Although Stalling claims he had nothing to do with the score of *Steamboat Willie*, there are indications that he did brush up Jackson's attempt.

Stalling spent less than two years with Disney, but his contributions were major in terms of techniques and approaches to synchronizing sound and action. His concept of the streamer, which is a line drawn on the film to simulate the musical beat, is another technique that is still used today when scoring a film.

In an interview in *Funnyworld*, Stalling recalled, "When I was composing the music for 'Gallopin' Gaucho' and 'Plane Crazy,' the two silent pictures, I had the cartoons shown at the theater where I worked, so that I could decide what music would be appropriate. I was having trouble figuring out how to get the music synchronized with the picture, then I hit on the idea of drawing 'half-moon' lines on the film that started on the left side of one frame, then moved to the right across the following frames, and then back toward the left, with the beat occurring when the line returned to the left side of the screen. That way, the beat didn't catch the musicians by surprise when we were recording..."

Another technique that Stalling developed was the tick system, or click-track, which also is still used today when recording a score. In the same *Funnyworld* interview Stalling explained, "The 'tick' was not really an invention, because it was not patentable. Perfect synchronization of music for cartoons was a problem since there were so many quick changes and actions that the music had to match. The thought struck me that if each member of the orchestra had a steady beat in their ear, from a telephone receiver, this would solve the problem. I had exposure sheets for the films with the picture broken down frame by frame, sort of like a script, and twelve of the film frames went through the projector in a half second. That gave us a beat....We made recordings of 'tick' sounds at different beats—a tick every eight frames, or ten frames or twelve frames—and played this on a phonograph connected to the recording machine and to earphones. Each member of the orchestra had a single earphone and listened to the clicks through that. It wasn't necessary for the conductor to give a beat, but I did, because one or two of the musicians didn't like to use the earphones."

With the overwhelming success of *Steamboat Willie* and the other two Mickey cartoons, the Disney studio expanded rapidly to meet the demand for the cartoon series. During the early Thirties, Disney was releasing a new Mickey Mouse cartoon every month. Each took about ten weeks to produce and could require as many as 125 people to finish it. At a cost of about $20,000, each cartoon ran approximately seven minutes in length.

Music played a role in each of the cartoons, although not a dominant one in most cases. The first song from the Disney studio was a theme song for Mickey, "Minnie's Yoo-Hoo," that was written in 1930 by Walt and Carl Stalling. This was Walt's only song credit, although he was extremely influential in all of the songs that were written for his pictures. Interestingly, the song enjoyed popularity again in the mid-Seventies as a disco number. The song is actually more of a ditty with these lyrics:

*I'm the guy they call little Mickey Mouse,*
*Got a sweetie down in the chicken house,*
*Neither fat nor skinny,*
*She's the horse's whinny,*
*She's my little Minnie Mouse.*

*When it's feeding time for the animals,*
*And they howl and growl like the cannibals,*
*I just turn my heel,*
*To the hen house steal,*
*And, you hear me sing this song.*

*Oh the old tom cat with his meow, meow, meow,*
*Old houn' dog with his bow, wow, wow,*
*The crow's caw, caw, and the mule's hee-haw*
*Gosh what a racket like an old buzz saw,*
*I have listened to the cuckoo kook his koo-koo,*
*And I've heard the rooster cock his doodle*
*    doo doo,*
*With the cows and the chickens,*
*They all sound like the dickens,*
*When I hear my little Minnie's yoo-hoo.*

*The Band Concert* in 1935 was probably the best use of music in a Mickey Mouse cartoon. Here Mickey made his Technicolor® debut, and Walt put him in a musical setting that resulted in one of the funniest and most classic cartoons ever made.

The film is centered on Mickey conducting an outdoor band concert in a performance of Rossini's *William Tell* overture. Into this virtuoso performance marches a noisy ice cream vendor, played by none other than Donald Duck, who proceeds to disrupt the concert, first with his voice, and then with an unending supply of fifes on which he plays "Turkey in the Straw." This naturally confuses the band, and the music skillfully rushes back and forth between the two numbers despite Mickey's valiant efforts as a conductor. As the band races toward the "storm" segment of the music, a real tornado approaches, and the result is the uninterrupted continuation of the music in the midst of the tornado. Visually and musically exciting, *The Band Concert* received rave reviews. One of the finest accolades came from the pre-eminent conductor Arturo Toscanini, who saw the film six times and invited Disney to visit him in Italy.

In a review in the *New Republic*, Otis Ferguson commented: "*The Band Concert* is a good reminder that...the musical staff at work on them (the cartoons) always seems to be well out front of other musical staffs in the industry. I do not mean for the mere synchronization and recording of sound, but for making sound a natural and basic part of the production, for originating scores and putting them over with good orchestral swing and nice handling of the vocal work—trios, choruses, or whatever. The music is light, but often fetching and always adequate, its function well understood."

*The Band Concert*, 1935.

Another Mickey cartoon that had a solid musical basis, and is an example of how music was used by Disney for comic effects, is *The Whoopee Party*, which was released in 1932. In it, Mickey and Minnie are throwing a house party which turns into a continuous musical sight gag. Minnie plays "Sweet Rosie O'Grady" on the piano, Mickey does "Maple Leaf Rag," and finally everyone joins in on "Running Wild." On that tune, Mickey uses mousetraps, window shades and household utensils for the percussion. All of the inanimate objects in the house join

in with the piano swaying and chairs, bureaus, coffee pots, etc. moving in time to the music. A long shot shows the whole house moving with the beat. When the police arrive, they also join in the fun.

Movie critic Leonard Maltin, in his excellent compendium *The Disney Films*, writes: "The whole cartoon moves to this music. Equally important, however, is what's happening on screen. *The Whoopee Party* is typical of the Mickey Mouse cartoons of this time. There is an incredible amount of action on the screen; an opening shot shows two couples dancing to the music. Later, when the party starts to jump, every single inch of the picture is filled with dancing figures. What is more, nothing is out of bounds for joining the fun: a pair of shirts on the ironing board are as likely to get up and dance as any of the animals at the party. The early Disney cartoons knew no limits when it came to such ideas; anything was fair game.''

Disney was extremely concerned that sound and music were an integral part of his productions and that the synchronization of sound and action was perfect. To accomplish this, the voices, music and sound effects were pre-recorded before the animation was finished. As Walt explained in an interview in *Scientific American*: "We always keep in mind the definite rhythm of music, even though the rhythm varies from time to time in the picture. We always score the background music before the picture is finished. Before we go into production we know the music to be used, the tempo and exact number of bars of each phrase to be played. Were we to finish the picture first, it would be impossible to bring sound effects, voices and music into perfect synchronization. If the effects vary one frame—1/24 of a second—we consider that to be an error; if they're two frames off, audiences will know there's something wrong, though only 1/12 of a second will be represented.''

Due to the technical limitations of the recording techniques available, the earlier cartoons required that sound and music be recorded simultaneously. This created additional concerns with the synchronization of sounds and action. As an example, if Pluto were to give a sniff on the 24th note of a measure,

*The Whoopee Party*, 1932.

one of the background musicians would have to inhale through one nostril on the 24th note. This inhalation, performed within inches of a microphone, would have to correspond with the exact frame on the picture where the dog begins to sniff.

This attention to precise detail and perfection is one of Disney's trademarks and, probably, a major reason for the success of his films. Dick Huemer, a story director at Disney who joined the studio as an animator in 1933, said in an interview in *Funnyworld*, "Disney never imagined taking the easy way out. That's certainly in my opinion one of the secrets of his success. Never to leave a thing until it had been milked in every possible way, and working it out in the best possible manner no matter how much time it took or how much money it cost. He built his pictures that way."

This concern for detail impressed Disney composer Paul Smith when he saw his first Mickey Mouse cartoon. He recalled: "Mickey was playing the piano and I noticed that the sound of the keys was perfectly matched to his finger action. But, what impressed me the most, he was playing the correct keys!"

Mickey Mouse enjoyed phenomenal success worldwide. Beginning in 1929, when the first merchandising license was granted to a pencil tablet manufacturer, the character of Mickey has been used for a myriad of merchandise items. Even today, telephones and watches with Mickey's likeness are

commonplace. In the early 1930's, with the country in the throes of a depression, the popularity of Mickey helped many struggling companies. L.H. Robbins, in a 1935 *New York Times Magazine* article, wrote: "New applause is heard for Mickey Mouse, rising high above the general acclaim for him that already rings throughout the earth. The fresh cheering is for Mickey the Big Business Man, the world's super-salesman. He finds work for jobless folk. He lifts corporations out of bankruptcy. Wherever he scampers, here or overseas, the sun of prosperity breaks through the clouds."

Walt closely identified with Mickey; in fact, for many years, Walt was the voice of Mickey Mouse. In later years, the studio's sound effects genius, Jimmy Macdonald, took over this role. Clarence Nash, the voice of Donald Duck, also substituted for Walt on some occasions when Walt was out of the country. In 1932, Walt was presented with a special Oscar for the "creation of Mickey Mouse."

The ultimate Mickey Mouse story was told by Charles Wolcott who was on Disney's musical staff in the Forties. Wolcott recalled that he and Disney were in New York near the end of World War II when Walt received a call. "Walt said that that was Washington calling. The Allied Forces were invading at Normandy and they wanted Walt to know that the password for the invasion was 'Mickey Mouse.' There were tears in Walt's eyes."

The evolution of Mickey Mouse.

*Opposite* (Top) Recording session — Two of Mickey's voices, Walt and Jimmy Macdonald (rear center). Clarence Nash (right) speaks for Donald. Rusty Jones assisted on sound effects.

(Bottom): Walt (center), Roy Disney (to the left of Walt), and staff in 1932 with the special Oscar for the "creation of Mickey Mouse."

# CHAPTER TWO

## *Experiments in Music: The* Silly Symphonies

The *Silly Symphony* series, inspired by Carl Stalling, represents the most important era of Disney film and music development. It was here that Disney and his staff experimented with new ways of using music and animation, developing and refining techniques such as the use of color and the multiplane camera that would be used so elegantly in later films. And, it was here that Disney had his first hit song, "Who's Afraid of the Big Bad Wolf?," which became a rallying cry for Americans suffering during the Depression.

Possibly one of the single most important characteristics of future Disney film-making sprung out of the creation of the *Silly Symphonies*—the dominant role that music would play in Disney films. This emphasis on music set a new precedent for how music and animation would interact within a film, a precedent that would influence how the later features would be developed. This commitment to building films around music greatly contributed to the enormous overall success of Disney studio productions.

This direction proved to be a natural one. As William Paul commented in *Movie*: "From its beginnings, film has had a natural affinity for music since both are art forms that move through time, but with cartoons, this affinity is more like symbiosis. It was inevitable that a perfect rhythmic synchronization of music and movement, 'mickey mousing,' the closest possible marriage of sound and image, should draw on cartoons for its name, since animation provides a total control that is closer to music than to live-action films."

The impetus for the *Silly Symphony* series came about through conflict between Walt and Stalling about the role of music in the Mickey Mouse cartoons. As Wilfred Jackson recalled in a *Funnyworld* interview: "Walt and Carl would time the pictures in Walt's office. Timing them consisted of working out what the music would be and what the action would be . . . . A lot of times Walt would want more time or less time for the action than could fit the musical phrase. So, there would be a pretty good argument going on in there. But, finally, Walt worked out a thing with Carl. He said, 'Look, let's work it out this way. We'll make two series. On the Mickey Mouse pictures, you make your music fit my action, the very best you can. But we'll make another series, and they'll be musical shorts. And in them music will take precedence and we'll adjust our action the best we can to what you think is the right music.'"

Stalling, in the same *Funnyworld* article, added: "After two or three of the Mickeys had been completed and were being run in theaters, Walt talked with me on getting started on the musical series I had in mind. When I told him I was thinking of inanimate figures, like skeletons, trees, flowers, etc., coming to life and dancing and doing other animated actions fitted to music more or less in a humorous and rhythmic mood, he became very interested. . . . For a name or title for the series, I suggested *not* using the word 'music' or 'musical,' as it sounded too commonplace, but to use the word

*The Skeleton Dance, 1929.*

'Symphony' together with a humorous word. At the next gag meeting, I don't know who suggested it, but Walt asked me: 'Carl, how would *Silly Symphony* sound to you?' I said, 'Perfect!' Then I suggested the first subject, 'The Skeleton Dance,' because ever since I was a kid I wanted to see real skeletons dancing and had always enjoyed seeing skeleton-dancing acts in vaudeville. As kids, we all like spooky pictures and stories, I think.''

As with many of the Disney films, the inspiration for them came from the childhood experiences of the people involved with them. In the case of the first *Silly Symphony*, Stalling recalled: '''The Skeleton Dance' goes way back to my kid days. When I was eight or ten years old, I saw an ad in *The American Boy* magazine of a dancing skeleton, and I got my dad to give me a quarter so I could send for it. It turned out to be a pasteboard cut-out of a loose-jointed skeleton, slung over a six-foot cord under the arm pits. It would 'dance' when kids pulled and jerked at each end of the string.''

For *The Skeleton Dance*, Stalling wrote an original score that was based on ''The March of the Dwarfs'' from Edvard Grieg's *Lyric Suite*. This was typical during the early days of the studio; adapting music in the public domain for use in Disney films. Doing this meant that Disney did not have to pay royalties for the use of the music. Since his profits were slim due to the perfection Walt demanded in his animation, any cost savings were welcome.

Once again Walt had to face an uphill struggle when he was ready to release *The Skeleton Dance* in 1929. When he submitted the film to the distributor of his Mickey Mouse cartoons, the response was ''Send more mice.'' Through perseverance, he was finally able to book the film into Los Angeles' Carthay Circle Theatre, where it opened to excellent reviews. Based on these reviews, he was able to convince the Roxy in New York, where *Steamboat Willie* had played, to take the film and it became an instant box office hit.

In an article in *Theatre Arts*, Hermine Rich Isaacs commented: ''In the first *Silly Symphony*, he (Walt) embarked upon a technique so revolutionary that no other producer has yet caught up with it. Instead of following established custom by using a score hastily written to order after the film was complete, and chopped up to order besides, he took an already written score and built the film around it. The result was a humorous animated ballet in which the characters were dictated by the musical score and moved in rhythm with it.''

Stalling left the studio in 1930. He later returned on a free-lance basis at Disney and worked on a dozen cartoons including *Three Little Pigs*, in which he played the piano for the third pig. Following Stalling's departure, Walt expanded his music staff and over the next three years added three composers who would make important contributions to the music of Disney—Frank Churchill, Leigh Harline, and Paul Smith.

Frank Churchill, who had done some previous recording work for Disney, joined the studio in 1931. He had studied music at UCLA and went on to such diverse endeavors as playing honky-tonk piano in Mexico to being a staff musician with a local Los Angeles radio station. According to those familiar with Churchill, he was adept at developing catchy melody lines for songs.

Leigh Harline, on the other hand, was proficient at developing lush orchestral arrangements. Harline had worked in radio before joining Disney in 1932. At the Disney studio, he worked on approximately 50 short subjects in addition to features. His work on *Pinocchio* won two Academy Awards—Best Song for ''When You Wish Upon A Star'' (in collaboration with Ned Washington) and Best Background Score (in collaboration with Paul Smith and Ned Washington).

In 1934, Paul Smith joined Disney, and like Churchill, he had studied music at UCLA. His music was versatile, ranging from catchy background scores for the cartoons to symphonic stylings in the *True-Life Adventure* series.

Many of the early Mickey Mouse cartoons and the Silly Symphonies did little more than take advantage of the novelty of their visual/musical combination. But as this initial novelty wore off, Disney

Frank Churchill

Paul Smith

Leigh Harline, Walt and Frank Churchill (left to right).

and his staff developed more sophisticated methods for coordinating images and sound. The music became more cohesive, with some of the Silly Symphonies becoming, in effect, one-act operettas, musical stage shows, vaudeville shows, concertos, and symphonic concerts.

The entire visual/musical process was complex. It wasn't simply the composer creating a musical score and then turning it over to the animators. Rather, composing the musical score for one of these *Silly Symphony* animated shorts involved painstaking collaboration between the composer and the film's director. The director was responsible for planning the continuity from the initial scenario and storyboard sketches, for the timing of individual scenes and shots, and for supervising the duration and placement of the music itself.

The director and composer worked together in what became known as the "music room." This was in fact the director's room with a piano so that the composer could work audibly with the music. Together the composer and director outlined the entire film, calculating its soundtrack, measure by measure, down to the fraction of a beat. They prepared the dope sheets which became complex diagrams and charts on which were recorded, prior to any animation, precise instructions on timing, music, dialogue and action. These dope sheets gave everyone a complete picture of the film.

Wilfred Jackson recalled his experiences in this collaborative effort in an interview in *Funnyworld*: "First, the musician would suggest tunes for the various sections of the picture to fit the mood or general type of action for each part. He would patiently play the same phrase over and over again while the animation director visualized and timed the action in his mind. Working back and forth, the musician would sometimes change elements in the score to enhance certain actions, or the director would modify some piece of business so that it worked better musically. When both were satisfied, the director would mark the action down on the dope sheet while his partner sketched out that part of the music score. Then they would move on to the next little piece of action. At last, when the action all the way

through the story had been pre-timed, a plan was achieved for both picture and sound. It was only after this timing had been finished, and after Walt had reviewed and okayed the plan, that the animators picked up their work."

Jackson added: "By the time Walt okayed the picture for animation, everything in it had been thoroughly worked and re-worked so as to guarantee the best result."

This entire process naturally required a great deal of cooperation between the composer and director. Even though music was of primary importance, consideration had to be given to the flow of the story. Jackson further said in the interview: "A song or dance number, or any other sequence which might need the animated action to be perfectly synchronized to the musical beat, naturally dictated that the score be composed and recorded first, usually as a vocal-piano or solo piano track to be fully orchestrated later. When the animation involved non-metered action or a gag situation of prime importance, and demanded that the animator be at least partially free to establish his own timing and visual rhythms, the animation itself took precedence and was post-scored."

A major technical breakthrough for Disney's cartoons occurred in 1932 with the *Silly Symphony Flowers and Trees*. Walt had long been intrigued with the idea of using color in his pictures, and when Technicolor perfected a process that looked promising for animation, Walt went forward. The short *Flowers and Trees*, a pastoral musical composition using the music of Mendelssohn and Schubert, had been half completed when Walt decided to re-do it in color. The film premiered at Grauman's Chinese Theater in Hollywood to rave reviews. From that point on, all of the Silly Symphonies were done in color, although it would be three years before Mickey was done in color.

*Flowers and Trees* was the first Disney film to win an award from the Academy of Motion Picture Arts and Sciences. During the next ten years, Disney cartoons would dominate the cartoon category, winning Academy Awards for: *Three Little Pigs* (1933); *The Tortoise and the Hare* (1935); *Three Orphan Kit-*

The Three Little Pigs sing ''Who's afraid of the big Bad Wolf?''

*Opposite:* Recording session for *Three Little Pigs* (1933) Walt (left) and, Frank Churchill at the piano, with singers Dorothy Compton, Pinto Colvig, and Mary Moder.

*tens* (1935); *Country Cousin* (1936); *The Old Mill* (1937); *Ferdinand the Bull* (1938); *The Ugly Duckling* (1939); *Lend a Paw* (1941); and, *Der Fuehrer's Face* (1943).

The next major Silly Symphony was *Three Little Pigs*. It featured Disney's first hit song, which was also the first hit song ever derived from a cartoon, "Who's Afraid of the Big Bad Wolf?"

As was the case with other Disney films, childhood memories played a role. In this case it involved the composer, Frank Churchill. While he was a boy on his father's ranch near San Luis Obispo, California, he had three pigs and he used to play the harmonica to them. One day, a wolf killed one of his pigs. In an interview published in *Author and Composer*, Churchill recalled: "Then one day Walt Disney came in with the idea for *Three Little Pigs*. It appealed to me instantly and, of course, it recalled my boyhood experience. . . .I thought it would be rather interesting to have the two little pigs playing flutes, and dancing about joyously, and contrasting these two with the one who worked hard all day."

Churchill claims he wrote the song in the short space of five minutes. The melody is loosely patterned after "Happy Birthday." Ted Sears, a writer in Disney's story department who had never written song lyrics before, contributed the lyrics: "I build my house of straw . . . I build my house of sticks . . . ." The chorus came naturally: "Who's afraid of the big bad wolf?" Ann Ronell later added lyrics to complete the song for the popular market.

Although everyone at the studio agreed the song was cute, no one anticipated its enormous popularity. When the film opened at New York's Radio City Music Hall, it attracted no more attention than any other Disney film. But when it reached the neighborhood theaters, the song became the rallying cry for a nation in the throes of the Depression. *Fortune*, a leading business journal, commented on the film: "First of all it is simple, at a time when all other entertainment in America's theaters is designed for a disillusioned audience. It gives pleasure; it appeals to your simplest emotions, whereas most other films cater to the complex emotions born of this troubled time."

Ross Care, who has written extensively about the early years of Disney music and composers, wrote in an article that appeared in *Funnyworld*: "The careful adherence of Churchill's scoring to the strict timing worked out beforehand by director Bert Gillett aided immeasurably in achieving a synthesis of plot, dialogue, and music that might justifiably be termed Wagnerian were not the adjective so vaunting in such a context. To present this little fable in the most direct and appealing of manners, song, rhymed speech and traditional background scoring were seamlessly wedded to musical gags. . . ."

Care added: "The plot unfolds purely through music, singing and rhythmically timed and spoken dialogue. It is a glorification of the Puritan work ethic, effected through the unlikely medium of a one-act cartoon operetta . . . its transposition posits each pig as an instrumentalist—flautist, fiddler, pianist—who delineates his own personality and presents the film's 'philosophy' (work and play don't mix) via song. Interestingly, the song 'Who's Afraid of the Big Bad Wolf?' is never rendered intact during the entire film, being fragmented, forestalled or interrupted by the narrative."

One person who saw the film and was impressed with the song was Sol Bourne, the general manager of Irving Berlin Music Company. Until this time, no one at Disney had considered using the songs as a means of promotion and revenue. Bourne acquired the music publishing rights for the song from Disney. Music publishers promote and plug songs, which in turn increases box-office appeal of a film. They also provide royalty income for the song's originator. This began a long relationship between Disney and Bourne, who later formed his own company when he and Irving Berlin separated. It was not until 1950 that Disney set up his own music publishing company, and although Disney reacquired the rights to some of the earlier music, Bourne still owns the songs published before 1941.

With the success of "Who's Afraid of the Big Bad Wolf?," the Disney music staff began writing more original songs for the Silly Symphonies. Harline and Churchill combined talents to write the melodic title song for *Lullaby Land* (1933). *The Grasshopper and the Ants* (1934) featured a delightful, catchy tune, "The World Owes Me a Living." In *The Flying Mouse* (1934), Churchill, in collaboration with a young scriptwriter, Larry Morey, wrote a bouncy song, "You're Nothin' but a Nothin'." In *Ferdinand the Bull* (1938), the music was written by Albert Hay Malotte, who joined the studio after achieving prominence for his moving composition, "The Lord's Prayer."

Throughout the Thirties, the Silly Symphony series challenged and inspired the imagination of Disney's staff. Experimentation was the key, since they were dealing with settings and situations that were uncharted, and they did not have established characters to fall back on.

An example of this is *Music Land* (1935), which is a "Romeo and Juliet" type of story featuring a saxophone who lives on the Isle of Jazz and a young violin who lives in the Land of Symphony. There is no dialogue in the picture, with all communication between the characters accomplished musically. In an interview in *Funnyworld*, the film's director Wilfred Jackson commented: "Back in the days when I was young, the imitation of spoken words with musical instruments was not too uncommon a vaudeville trick. And too, when the musicians at Disney got together to warm up and tune their instruments for one of our recording sessions, they would sometimes clown around 'talking' to one another with musical sounds: a tuba player might make sudden, fierce, growling sounds at a violinist, who would squeal back with 'frightened' squeaks from his fiddle."

These techniques were used to their fullest in *Music Land*. Organs, strings, and harps were used to characterize Symphony Land. Brass, saxes, reeds, and wild drum riffs were used to characterize Isle of Jazz sequences. In one humorous sequence, the sax is imprisoned in Symphony Land's metronome prison and writes a letter for help, notating it on a sheet of musical manuscript paper. As he writes, each of his "notes" is played by a studio musician. When he makes a visible writing mistake, the musician "flubs" the note. It is then erased and rewritten and the musician picks up with the right note.

Another outstanding Silly Symphony was *The Old Mill*, which was totally a musical extravaganza

The 1935 Silly Symphony *Music Land.*

and represented the first use of a Disney technical development—the multiplane camera—that would be used so effectively in *Pinocchio*. *The Old Mill* was presented in four parts. The first part consists of the camera slowly moving in on the old mill and its inhabitants during the quiet of sunset. The second is a comedy sequence featuring a group of frogs in the pond. A nighttime storm ravages the mill and its inhabitants in the third sequence. Finally, the storm passes and the mill community returns to its peaceful setting at dawn.

Leigh Harline composed the music for this Academy Award-winning classic. Ross Care, writing in *Film Music Notebook*, states: "The Old Mill contains what is probably the finest, most lavish original score ever composed expressly for a short film. Here, the entire action proceeds in intimate conjunction with Harline's haunting score which, if detached from the visuals, forms a perfectly structured, self-contained four-movement tone poem (somewhat similar in form to a romantic overture such as Rossini's William Tell) and one which is analogous to the four 'movements' of the film itself."

Through the years, musical cartoons continued to be the vehicle for experimentation at Disney. Although production of them declined during the Forties, there were two notable films released in 1953—*Melody* and *Toot, Whistle, Plunk and Boom*—both directed by C. August Nichols and Ward Kimball. Kimball joined the Disney staff as a animator in 1934 and had a musical background; he was an enthusiastic trombonist and jazz aficionado. In 1948 he organized a Dixieland Jazz group, the Firehouse Five Plus Two, which featured Disney artists and musicians. The group produced 12 record albums between 1950 and 1970.

*Melody* was Disney's first 3-D film. The other short, *Toot, Whistle, Plunk and Boom*, won an Academy Award and was the first cartoon to be produced in CinemaScope® . Both films dealt with various aspects of music theory and history in a typically Disney manner.

Commenting on the Silly Symphony series in a 1936 issue of *Stage* magazine, Marcia Davenport, in an article aptly titled "Not so Silly," writes: "There is delicious artlessness in the name that Walt Disney has given to his animations of beloved nursery tales, Silly Symphonies! For one thing, they are more sage than silly, and for another, the music which bears out the title is not silly, even when the pictures are. It is, this music, about as expert and judicious a rendition of functional music as you can hear anywhere. Its rhythm is better than that of the strains to which musical comedy artists dance and sing, and its compactness and cohesion can show grand opera a thing or two. Most of it is composed especially for the pictures in which it is heard, and is not distinguished by any great originality of theme. But it has a remarkable way of reflecting and suggesting the content and sequence of the story—which is what such music is supposed, and too often fails, to do."

*Melody* (1953) — Disney's first 3-D film.

*Opposite:* (Top) *Toot, Whistle, Plunk and Boom* (1953) was the first cartoon to be produced in CinemaScope.

(Bottom): Ward Kimball (with trombone) and the Firehouse Five Plus Two (top row, left to right): Dick Roberts, Frank Thomas, and Danny Alguire; (bottom row, left to right): Ward Kimball, Jim Macdonald, George Probert, and George Bruns.

# CHAPTER THREE

## *The Successful Folly:* Snow White

**S**now *White and the Seven Dwarfs* was Walt's personal masterpiece. Although Walt was involved in all of his studio's productions, *Snow White* completely engrossed him. He developed the story-line continuity, described in minute detail what each scene would involve, suggested what lyrics should be used in songs, selected the songs to be used, cast the voices, and lived and breathed the film for the more than three years that it was in production. As composer Paul Smith, who worked on the background score for the film, recalled: "Occasionally you really fall in love with a film. In my case, it was *Cinderella.* Walt's great love was *Snow White.*"

Because of his total commitment to the film and story, Walt was never quite satisfied with the result. He told a reporter just before the film's release in 1937: "I've seen so much of *Snow White*, I'm only conscious of the places where it can be improved... I wish I could yank it back and do it all again." Nevertheless, *Snow White* has become a classic; and fifty years later is still enjoyably delightful.

*Snow White* was born out of Walt's basic hunger for a new challenge after the success of the Silly Symphonies. This was a pattern that would repeat itself throughout his life, since he thrived on new fields to conquer. His next challenge was to produce a feature-length animated film, something no one else in the industry had ever attempted before. When Walt's plans for *Snow White* were revealed, Hollywood insiders promptly dubbed it "Disney's Folly." There was a general consensus that audiences would not sit through a feature-length cartoon.

This was not the first time that Walt had considered producing a full-length feature, however. According to studio historians, in the early 1930s Mary Pickford wanted him to produce a feature length *Alice in Wonderland* in which she would star as Alice, but all of the other characters would be animated. Disney recalled in 1937 that "she was going to put up the money. . . . It wouldn't have been too difficult in black and white—just a lot of intricate process shots. I worked out a plan. Then Paramount came along with a production of *Alice* (in late 1933), and that knocked out our idea."

Also during the early 1930s, Disney revealed, he and Will Rogers conferred on a feature-length version of Rip Van Winkle, with the little men to be done in animation and Rogers portraying Rip. However, Paramount wouldn't release its rights to the famous play that was based on the novel.

The roots for *Snow White and the Seven Dwarfs* went back to Walt's childhood. As he recalled: "When I was a child, every evening after supper, my grandmother would take down from the shelf the well-worn volumes of Grimms' fairy tales and Hans Christian Andersen. It was the best time of the day for me, and the stories and characters in them seemed quite as real as my schoolmates and our games. Of all the characters in the fairy tales, I loved Snow White best, and when I planned my first full-length cartoon, she inevitably was the heroine."

If it was a challenge that Disney craved, then a full-length feature was just the project to satisfy his appetite. Producing a feature wasn't simply a matter of stringing together a series of animated vignettes. It was an extremely complex endeavor, requiring new disciplines than those associated with the six-to-eight minute cartoons. First, a story outline was developed. Then, a storyline was created that would have both continuity and the ability to sustain the audience's interest and attention. The storyline would be broken down into separate sequences, and story boards for each sequence were developed and refined. Songs were then planned and written, and a background score was outlined. And naturally, during the entire process, each element was subject to change. Even after the animation and scoring had been completed, sequences would be changed or actually dropped.

As Jon Newsom noted in his chapter "A Sound Idea: Music for Animated Films," which appeared in the Library of Congress' *Wonderful Inventions*, there is a distinct difference in composing music for an animated film compared with a live-action film. He wrote: "The differing techniques of producing an animated, as opposed to a live-action film, call for correspondingly different working relationships between directors and composers—not to mention the many others whose special skills contribute to the art of animation. This is true because of the relatively complex microcosmic planning required for animated films, for which the sight and sound elements of each frame must be accounted before filming . . . . In live-action films, perhaps one-tenth of the film exposed is used in the final print and, even after the composer's carefully synchronized work has been recorded and dubbed on the sound track, large cuts may be made. Then, at best, the composer may have the chance to recompose, rearrange and rerecord his score to fit the new editing. At worst, his score may be mangled and discarded. But such cutting and editing are rarely done in animated films. And, in some cases, though by no means as a rule, the composer's score, together with voices and sound effects, may be recorded before the film has been animated."

The complexity of the feature-length animated film required that a new approach to music be taken. With the shorts, the composer would write the songs, if needed, and provide the background score. For the feature however, an arranger and orchestrator were also now required. The arranger would work from a song's basic version, usually a piano "lead" sheet which would just provide the melody line of the song, to create a more polished version. He would coordinate with the animation director and story men to work out the timing so that the music related to the visual's rapid changes in mood and tempo.

The orchestrator would work in one of two ways. If he were provided only with an expanded lead sheet, he would be responsible for structuring the entire instrumental portion for the songs and develop the background score to provide the sounds, colors, and effects that enhance a film. In other cases, the composer's or arranger's score would be complete, including specific instrumental instructions as to solo lines, accompaniment, and countermelodies. Then, the orchestrator would technically complete the score by detailing the instrumental ranges, transpositions, effects, and phrasings so that the score would work orchestrally with the film.

The man most responsible for the music in *Snow White* was Frank Churchill, who had the dual role of composer and arranger, writing the songs and providing the arrangements for them. With an independent spirit, he had the reputation of being the "Peck's Bad Boy" of the Disney music staff. Frank Thomas and Ollie Johnston in *Disney Animation* recall: "Walt used to claim that Frank Churchill always slept through the story meetings and never listened to his first instructions, but Frank hardly can be blamed. He knew that no matter what ideas were tossed out, and no matter how enthusiastically they might be received, that would have little bearing on the music he eventually would write . . . . He figured, correctly, that he would do better to wait until the decisions had been made and the footage set, and then he could write a score with integrity and flow, regardless of what had happened to the so-called structure. He would sit at his piano penciling in his melodies and muttering, 'This note is for the director, and this is for the producer, while this little note down here is for the animator, and this is for the director's Aunt Tilda, and this is just for me!' "

Leigh Harline and Paul Smith were also important to the development of the music for *Snow White* as orchestrators for sequences of the film. Harline did the scoring for certain sections of the film, such as the eerie music for the "Magic mirror on the wall" sequence, the ominous background music for the laboratory scene, and the dwarfs' pursuit of the queen. As Jon Newsom notes: "If Churchill's greatest strength was as a composer of melodies, Leigh Harline's was as Disney's 'Symphonist,' silly or otherwise, and his talents led him to dramatic orchestral scoring for some of Disney's finest shorts and features."

From the beginning, *Snow White* was planned as a musical extravaganza. In an early story conference outline from August 1934, a number of song possibilities are outlined including "Some Day My Prince Will Come," which became one of the big song hits from the film. Frank Churchill and Larry Morey reportedly wrote twenty-five songs for the film, with eight finally being used. Three of *Snow White*'s eight songs—"Heigh-Ho," "Whistle While You Work," and "Some Day My Prince Will Come"—became major song hits on radio and recordings. Two others—"One Song" and "With a Smile and a Song"—also enjoyed a degree of popularity. As was the case with several animation sequences, songs were planned and written and later dropped by Walt in an effort to have his studio produce the best film possible.

Musically, *Snow White* presents the finest example of the total creative integration of film and music, and it is better constructed than any musical picture of that era. It was Disney's objective that the songs would either offer exposition, develop characters and situations, or advance the plot rather than be musical interludes randomly inserted in the film. During the early stages of planning, Walt directed his staff to create music that would fit the film. He said: "It still can be good music and not follow the same pattern everybody in the country has followed. We still haven't hit in any of these songs . . . .It's still the influence from the musicals they have been doing for years. Really, we should set a new pattern, a new way to use music—weave it into the story so somebody doesn't just burst into song."

Snow White sings "I'm Wishing."

*Opposite:* "Whistle While You Work."

The film opens with a musical rendition of "Some Day My Prince Will Come" as an old-fashioned storybook is used on the screen to establish the background of the main character. When the audience first meets Snow White, she is working in the garden. As she goes to the well to fill her wash pail, she sings "I'm Wishing":

*I'm wishing for the one I love to find me today.*
*I'm hoping,*
*And I'm dreaming of the nice things, he'll say.*
*Ah, I'm wishing for the one I love to find me*
*    today.*

The Prince overhears her song and joins in on the last line. Snow White flees and the Prince stands under her balcony and sings *"One song, I have but one song. One song—only for you."* The action changes as the wicked queen sends Snow White into the woods along with the huntsman who is ordered to kill her. During this sequence, Paul Smith builds the feeling of suspense and danger with muted French horns to symbolize the approaching huntsman. The compassionate huntsman allows Snow White to escape, during which Smith's music is frantic and builds to a whirlwind finish. Snow White falls exhausted to the ground and the music becomes a light, spring-like melody as the animals emerge from hiding to find her.

One of the most delightful sequences of the film is when Snow White discovers the dwarfs' cottage, is appalled by the untidiness and begins to clean it with the help of her animal friends. Here she sings one of the most popular songs from the film:

*Just whistle while you work. (whistle)*
*And cheerfully together we can tidy up the place.*
*So hum a merry tune. (hum)*
*It won't take long when there's a song*
*To help you set the pace.*
*And as you sweep the room*
*Imagine that the broom is someone that*
*    you love*
*And soon you'll find you're dancing to the tune.*
*When hearts are high*
*The time will fly*
*So whistle while you work.*

Always striving for the perfect marriage of music and animation, Disney's comments during a story conference concerning the "Whistle While You Work" sequence of the film demonstrate his creativity and intense involvement with each and every element of his productions: "Change the words of the song so they fit in more with Snow White's handing the animals brushes, etc. . . . Snow White: 'If you just hum a merry tune'—and they start humming . . . . Then Snow White would start to tell them to 'whistle while you work.' She would start giving the animals things to do. By that time, she has sung, of course . . . . Birds could come marching in. Try to arrange to stay with the birds for a section of the whistling . . . . Get it in the woodwinds—like playing something instrumentally to sound like whistling . . . . Get a way to finish the song that isn't just an end. Work in a shot trucking out of the house. Truck back and show animals shaking rugs out of the windows—little characters outside beating things out in the yard. Truck out and the melody of 'Whistle While You Work' gets quieter and quieter. Leave them all working— birds scrubbing clothes. The last thing you see as you truck away is little birds hanging clothes. Fade out on that and music would fade out—at the end all you would hear is the flute—before fading into the Dig, Dig song ("Heigh-Ho") and the hammering rhythm."

Jon Newsom added in his "A Sound Idea: Music for Animated Films": "The 'Whistle While You Work' sequence moves smoothly from dialogue through spoken song text, to the actual singing, with the orchestral accompaniment gradually developing the musical atmosphere. By the time Snow White and her forest helpers begin to sing as they clean up the dwarfs' cottage, their song seems like a natural continuation of the preceding spoken dialogue. The songs are thoroughly integrated and dramatically well placed, but they also stand on their own, and *Snow White* may claim more enduring popular tunes than any other Disney film."

Every action in the film is built around a musical beat. For example, the dwarfs are introduced with a steady, march-type dirge, "We dig, dig, dig." This naturally flows into "Heigh-Ho":

*We dig-dig-dig-dig-dig-dig-dig in our mine the*
  *whole day through,*
*To dig-dig-dig-dig-dig-dig-dig is what we like to do,*
*It ain't no trick*
*To get rich quick*
*If ya' dig-dig-dig*
*With a shovel or a pick.*
*In a mine*
*In a mine*
*In a mine*
*In a mine*
*Where a million diamonds shine.*
*We dig-dig-dig-dig-dig-dig-dig*
*From early morn till night.*
*We dig-dig-dig-dig-dig-dig-dig*
*Up ev'rything in sight.*
*We dig up diamonds by the score*
*A hundred rubies—sometimes more*
*Though we don't know what we dig 'em for*
*We dig-dig-dig-dig-dig!*

*"Heigh-ho," "Heigh-ho,"*
*It's home from work we go. (whistle)*
  *"Heigh-Ho,"*
*"Heigh-Ho," "Heigh-Ho," "Heigh-Ho,"*
  *"Heigh-Ho,"*
*It's home from work we go. (whistle)*
*"Heigh-Ho," "Heigh-Ho,"*

During this sequence, each dwarf is in step and their footsteps are in perfect time with the musical beat. The characterization of the dwarfs is brilliant. From the befuddled Doc to the childlike innocence of Dopey, the characters are wonderfully endearing. Each dwarf has his own musical theme, and when all are together, the theme has seven notes. In the "Dwarfs' Yodel Song," there is a strong temptation to jump up and join them in a polka. Surprisingly, buried in the background of the score is a melody line that resembles "Supercalifragilisticexpialidocious," which would not emerge on its own until *Mary Poppins* (1964).

In another sequence of the film, Grumpy plays a wheezy, old organ. To achieve the sound for the organ, the imagination of sound effects creator Jim Macdonald was truly tested. He came up with the idea of having studio personnel blow into large jugs.

The sounds that Grumpy produces on the old organ were created by having studio personnel blow into large jugs.

As animators Frank Thomas and Ollie Johnston recall: "With considerable ingenuity and a great deal of blowing and accompanying dizziness, a track had been recorded for the organ that Grumpy played in the dwarfs' house. It was only a first test, but it involved everyone in the studio who could read music, plus a handful of competent musicians and all the sound effects men, some thirty of us in all, blowing on bottles and jugs and strange homemade instruments. The most demanding part was for the man who blew over the giant jug for the lowest bass notes. That part had gone to Jim."

Following these lighthearted and merry sequences with the dwarfs, the tone of the film changes as the wicked queen reappears to tempt Snow White with a deadly apple. The curse on the apple cannot be broken except by love's first kiss. The dwarfs dispose of the queen, and the prince arrives to wake Snow White from her deathlike sleep. And, they live happily ever after.

Throughout the creation of the film, Walt demonstrated over and over his uncanny ability to visualize the impact that the music could have on the mood of a particular sequence. For example, in a story conference concerning the sequence in which Snow White is tempted with the poisoned apple, he suggested: "The thought just struck me on the build-up of the music to where she says 'now turn red,' etc., that where it starts, you might go into innocent sweet music while she is saying something about how innocent it looks. Instead of saying how it will tempt Snow White. The music changes as the apple changes and could stay that way until she says: 'Have a bite.' It would be a good contrast."

*Snow White and the Seven Dwarfs* premiered at the Carthay Circle Theater in Los Angeles on

December 21, 1937, and it was an instant success for the struggling Disney Studio. Produced at a cost of approximately $1.5 million—an unheard-of-figure for a cartoon—it grossed more than $8 million. The funds enabled Walt to begin building a new studio in Burbank. More important, it proved that there was a market for feature-length animated films, and it gave added impetus to two other projects in production—*Fantasia* and *Pinocchio*. And, it silenced his Hollywood critics who had labeled *Snow White* "Disney's Folly."

The background score by Harline, Churchill, and Smith was nominated for an Academy Award. A year later, Walt was presented with a special Oscar for *Snow White* "recognized as a significant screen innovation which has charmed millions and pioneered a great new entertainment field for the motion picture cartoon." Shirley Temple presented the award to Walt — an Oscar accompanied by seven little Oscars.

With the incredible success of *Snow White*, Disney's distributors responded with pleas to "send more dwarfs." Walt had produced sequels to the *Three Little Pigs* at the urging of his distributors to "send more pigs," but none matched the vitality of the original. Walt was not one to repeat himself, instead preferring to charge forward toward new challenges. Also, Walt had a keen sense of which subjects would work with animated films and which would not. As he told Cecil B. DeMille in an interview in 1938: "Never do anything that someone else can do better. That's why I ordinarily sidestep stories that could be done successfully in live action instead of animated action."

The importance of *Snow White* is further evidenced by the fact that the Disney organization re-releases the film approximately every five to seven years. It is one of the few Disney films that has not been generally released for use on television or to the home video market.

The premiere of *Snow White and the Seven Dwarfs* at the Carthay Circle Theater in Los Angeles, December 21, 1937.

*Opposite:* Review that appeared in the February 12, 1938 edition of the Los Angeles Liberty.

Liberty — Feb. 12, 1938

# "Disney's Folly" Makes History

## A Grimm fairy tale comes to life as something new under the sun . . Hollywood laughs at Hollywood, with music

### ★ ★ ★ ★ SNOW WHITE AND THE SEVEN DWARFS

Based on the fairy tale by the Brothers Grimm. Produced by Walt Disney for release by RKO-Radio Pictures. Running time, 82 minutes.*

THIS is Walt Disney's dream come true. For years he has hoped to make a feature-length film, a wholly animated production without human actors.

Snow White has a rare and elusive charm. It is a lovely translation of the old fairy tale created by Jakob Ludwig Grimm and Wilhelm Karl Grimm—the fantasy of the beautiful little princess who flees her wicked stepmother and comes to dwell in the depths of the forest with the seven dwarfs who labor by day in a jewel mine.

But the stepmother consults her magic mirror, summons all her black wiles, and sets out to kill the little princess.

Like all Germanic folk tales, Snow White has its vein of cruelty. It has fearsome things reaching out of the forest darkness to terrorize the fleeing Snow White; it has its horrible witch with her lust for blood. But the fable also has its beauty, its humor, its tenderness.

The birds, the squirrels, the forest hares, the fawns, all the shy folk of the woodland, do their best to help Snow White. Here the film achieves a lyric loveliness impossible to any-

* Recommended for children.

### By BEVERLY HILLS

READING TIME ● 8 MINUTES 7 SECONDS

4 STARS—EXTRAORDINARY
3 STARS—EXCELLENT     2 STARS—GOOD
1 STAR—POOR      0 STAR—VERY POOR

thing of flesh and blood. Too, the fantasy, unbelievable as it may seem, possesses its tense and moving moments.

The dwarfs are individual and delightfully characterized, quaint little beings of fantasy.

Snow White is something brand-new under the Hollywood sun.

VITAL STATISTICS: Story's been left much as the Grimm Bros.—Jakob Ludwig & Wilhelm Karl—conceived it late in the 19th century. Chief differences: Animals and birds have been given human characteristics, dwarfs have been named Sleepy, Sneezy, Grumpy, Happy, Bashful, Dopey, and Doc and characterized sharply. Squatty, by the way, is a ringer for Dopey but wears a beard. Grimm Bros. won undying fame but few riches. . . . Snow White's been 4 years in the making, tying with Chaplin's Modern Times for the longevity production record. Hollywood called it Disney's Folly. At world premeer, however, all Hollywood paid $5.50 a ticket, cheered Disney, speculators got $50 a seat. . . . Disney artists are known as Disney's hands, work for from $19 a week to about $350 tops. . . . None of the offstage voices in Snow White get credit, are sworn by contract to secrecy as to their identity, ride around in comfortable cars nevertheless. . . . Walter Elias Disney is a 1-goal-handicap polo player, loves his 2 children to distraction, is happily and once married, he's

of Chicago birth and Missouri farm upbreeding. Studied drawing at Chicago night schools, was turned down for ill health when he applied as a postman in Chicago, went home, put on make-up and got the job. Spent two years driving a Red Cross war ambulance in France. His first art job was drawing farmyard animals for a Kansas City ad agency. While working nights over a drawing board a fat mouse ran out, made friends with him, got named Mortimer Mouse, later became Mickey Mouse after quite a struggle to crash world of animation.

### ★ ★ ★ HOLLYWOOD HOTEL

THE PLAYERS: Dick Powell, Rosemary Lane, Lola Lane, Ted Healy, Hugh Herbert, Johnnie Davis, Glenda Farrell, Alan Mowbray, Louella Parsons, Frances Langford, Mabel Todd, Ken Niles, Jerry Cooper, Allyn Joslyn, Duane Thompson, Edgar Kennedy, Grant Mitchell, Curt Bois, Fritz Feld, Eddie Acuff, Perc Westmore, Sarah Edwards, Clinton Rosemond, Wally Maher, William Davidson, Libby Taylor, Georgia Cooper, Paul Irving, Joe Romantini, Raymond Paige, Benny Goodman. Screen play by Jerry Wald, Maurice Leo, and Richard Macauley from a story by Mr. Wald and Mr. Leo. Directed by Busby Berkeley. Produced by Warner Brothers. Running time, 95 minutes.*

BUILT around Louella Parsons' well known radio hour, this is entertaining—and far too long.

The action centers around the imaginary Orchid Room of the equally fabulous Hollywood Hotel and shows a broadcast wherein the jobless would-be movie actor Ronnie Bowers (otherwise Dick Powell) goes on in an emergency and makes a great hit. The picture, too, delves into the secrets of picture making (if there are any secrets left) and laughs heartily at Hollywood.

Miss Parsons is completely herself

* Recommended for children.

**Snow White and her forest friends, as they appear in Walt Disney's success.**

# CHAPTER FOUR

## *A Musical Fantasy:* Fantasia

The word "fantasia" in musical terms means a free development of a given theme. For Disney, *Fantasia* was the ultimate in experimenting with music, because here music is visualized. In his early films, especially the *Silly Symphonies*, music had a dominant role. But in *Fantasia*, music ruled. Never again would Disney produce a film of this musical scope. For generations of American movie-goers, the film marked the first time many of them ever had even been exposed to classical music. In describing *Fantasia* to his staff, Disney said: "We are picturing music. This music is not serving as background to a picture."

Leopold Stokowski, the world-renowned conductor of the Philadelphia Orchestra who was intimately involved with all aspects of the film from its very beginning, wrote in the foreword of Deems Taylor's book, *Fantasia*: "In making *Fantasia*, the music has suggested the mood, the coloring, the design, the speed, the character of motion of what is seen on the screen. Disney and all of us who work with him believe that for every composition there are beautiful pictures. Music by its nature is in constant motion, and this movement can suggest the mood of the picture it invokes.

"*Fantasia* was created and drawn by artists most of whom have no knowledge of, or training in, music. As enthusiastic listeners, they've been able to penetrate the inner character of the music and discover depths of expression that sometimes have been missed by musicologists."

Disney commented on the film: "In a profession that has been an unending voyage of discovery in the realms of color, sound and motion, *Fantasia* represents our most exciting adventure. At last we have found a way to use in our medium the great music of all times and the flood of new ideas which it inspires. Perhaps Bach and Beethoven are strange bedfellows for Mickey Mouse, but it's all been a lot of fun."

*Fantasia* had its beginnings in 1937 when Disney acquired the rights to use Paul Dukas' "Sorcerer's Apprentice" as the basis for an animated cartoon. With *The Sorcerer's Apprentice* Disney was looking for something different. He wanted to use existing music that had its own storyline. Another consideration, according to Disney archivist David R. Smith, was that Walt wanted some added prestige for the project by using a well-known name as musical conductor.

Walt saw Stokowski by coincidence at a Hollywood restaurant where the idea for *The Sorcerer's Apprentice* took root. As Jon Newsom relates: "Stokowski recalls meeting Disney unexpectedly in a restaurant and conversing as follows: 'He told me about a French composition about a kind of a great magician and a bad boy. He liked that music very much and so we discussed it . . . .He said 'You know—how would you like the idea of making a picture of that? I have some thoughts of how that magician looked and how the bad boy looked, and it is very picturesque, brilliant music.' So gradually we decided to do it and it was completed. Then we looked at it together when it was all finished and Disney said, 'I think we should add that to some other things and make a long picture of regular length.'"

This initial encounter with Disney excited Stokowski. Although renowned as a classical music conductor, Stokowski was no stranger to Hollywood. He had worked on several films, including Paramount's *The Big Broadcast of 1937*, and also had an abiding interest in putting classical music to film. In 1936, he had written in *Etude*: "For it seems to us high time that we begin to help to realize the great possibilities of the present-day sound film for multiplying the audience for the world's richest and most satisfying music . . . .I have been called 'experimental,' 'daring,'and even 'sensational.' In short, I tried to make the best music and the public taste meet, to the mutual benefit of both."

Mickey Mouse seemed to be the logical choice for the title role in *The Sorcerer's Apprentice*. It was likely that Walt wanted to find something for Mickey that would be akin to the success his Silly Symphonies were enjoying yet would not be typical Mickey Mouse cartoon antics. It's also possible he was looking at this film as a means of upgrading Mickey's image.

*The Sorcerer's Apprentice* was to be unlike any other Mickey Mouse cartoon. As the film's animation director, Perce Pearce, noted: "With Mickey as 'The Apprentice,' we will match to the music a fantasy designed as a faithful pictorial adaptation of the original musical composition. The picture presents an opportunity to achieve a new high in imaginative quality . . . .The picture will be made without dialogue and without sound effects, depending solely on pantomime and descriptive music."

Stokowski recorded the soundtrack for *The Sorcerer's Apprentice* in Hollywood using studio musicians. Later, he would record the remainder of the score to *Fantasia* conducting his own Philadelphia Orchestra. When *The Sorcerer's Apprentice* was finished, this nine-minute musical cartoon had cost nearly $125,000 to produce, and with little prospect of recouping the investment by releasing it as a short, Disney turned to the idea that he and Stokowski had discussed about doing an entire film based on concert music. In 1938, the two impresarios and Deems Taylor, a noted composer and critic, began selecting the music that would eventually make up *Fantasia*.

*Fantasia* did not have to go through the tedious and time-consuming process that other animated

Walt with Leopold Stokowski.

features experience, since the film would be composed of independent vignettes that were only interrelated through the music. Therefore, there wasn't that process that occurred in *Snow White* where major sequences were animated and then abandoned. (Although "Clair de Lune" was animated and then dropped, it was later used with different music as the "Blue Bayou" sequence of *Make Mine Music*.)

As Jimmy Johnson, who later was to help establish the Walt Disney Music Company, recalled: "In making a film like *Pinocchio*, Walt would give the various sequences to individual directors depending on their ability to handle comic characters . . . even though the director's styles were different, it was all the same story and there had be to a unity about it. With *Fantasia* it was different, the various sequences really bore no relation to one another except they were part of the same concert. So Walt's casting was more in the direction of different art styles, though action and characters were important too in some sequences."

The film is a delight of contrasting visual interpretations of music. To create the feeling of a live concert, *Fantasia* opens with Deems Taylor walking onto the stage to introduce the film. He reappears throughout the original version introducing each sequence and number, and again during the filmed intermission.

Commenting on the structure of the film, Hermine Rich Isaacs, writing in *Theatre Arts*, notes: "The framework for the picture provides many surprises, and some of the gayest moments of all. Photographed from varied camera angles in silhouette with the subtlest suggestion of color, the Philadelphia Orchestra musicians are shown tuning up before each movement; Deems Taylor gives a short introduction, Leopold Stokowski mounts the podium, raises his baton, and the performance begins. But interlaced with these more or less ordinary preparations for the concert is a series of mad spoofs that keep things rolling in an uproarious vein. There is a jam session before the Pastoral Symphony

which, rumor has it, was inserted while Mr. Stokowski was in South America. At one point the sound track itself shyly appears on the screen for one of the hit performances of the show. Another time an appropriately cacophonous prelude to Stravinsky's 'Rite of Spring' is supplied when the gong player suddenly upsets his instrument. These are but a few of the many bright moments that illuminate the performance.''

The first number in the film is Bach's "Toccata and Fugue in D Minor," which is comprised of seemingly random visual patterns such as waves, concentric circles, and beams of light forming and reforming in time with the music.

The second number, Tchaikovsky's "Nutcracker Suite," features fairies, mushrooms, petals, fish, thistles, and flowers performing dances corresponding to each of the six movements. Next is Mickey in "The Sorcerer's Apprentice" where he is inundated with water as his conjured brooms pay little heed to his protestations. At the conclusion of this sequence, Mickey appears on stage with Stokowski to congratulate him.

This is followed by Stravinsky's "Rite of Spring," where the Disney staff interpreted the music as representing the creation of life. Microscopic particles open the number, with dinosaurs and other prehistoric creatures following in later sequences. Many critics objected to this sequence, as interpreted by Disney, because they felt it did not reflect the intent of the music.

Differing viewpoints of how music should be interpreted was one of the areas of controversy for *Fantasia*. But as Isaacs points out in *Theatre Arts*: "Here then is the obstacle that *Fantasia's* creators meet and do not entirely conquer in their pioneering effort: they are faced with an audience familiar with the musical score, and with many preconceived notions about it which *Fantasia*, with its own notions, cannot dispel. Every person who has heard the pieces has a definite idea of their interpretation, and although his conception sometimes coincides with Disney's, more often it does not. Where Stravinsky's 'Rite of Spring' suggested the story of evolution to the filmmakers, to some of the listeners it is more suggestive of orgiastic dancing and festivals of springtime, and to others it is absolute music that cannot be interpreted in literal terms.''

Following the "Rite of Spring" is a filmed intermission with its own set of musical pranks. At the start of the intermission, the string bass player plucks out a jazz beat. Before long, there is a full-scale jam session in progress. When Deems Taylor returns to the stage, a frowning look quickly brings the musicians to a halt, and Taylor introduces one of the unsung stars of the concert—the sound track. Although timid at first, it comes on camera and shows the audience how it reproduces various sounds from the orchestra such as the harp, bassoon, flute, and trumpet. At the end of the intermission there is a jazz solo by the drummer and a final chime from a triangle, which creates a triangular shape on the track.

Following the intermission was Beethoven's "Pastoral Symphony," which had a Greek motif complete with unicorns, centaurs, and nymphs. In the next sequence, one of the more unusual ballets on film was performed by hippos, elephants, ostriches, and alligators in Ponchielli's "Dance of the Hours." The finale presented a musical counterpoint with Moussorgsky's ominous "Night on Bald Mountain" and Schubert's ethereal "Ave Maria."

Disney considered *Fantasia* to be a very special film, and he wanted it to be the best possible presentation of music. Yet, he knew that current film sound systems were inadequate to properly convey the majesty of the music. So, in typical Disney fashion, Walt designed his own sound system that would make his picture better. Under Walt's direction, the Disney staff worked with RCA sound engineers to develop an elaborate sound system, Fantasound, that would revolutionize the industry's approach to music sound recording, and would become the forerunner of today's more exotic sound systems. In 1941, the Motion Picture Academy presented Disney and RCA with a special award in recognition of Fantasound and "for their outstanding contributions to the advancement of the use of sound in motion pictures through the production of *Fantasia*." Stokowski received a special Oscar that was presented to him "and his associates for their unique achievement in the creation of a new form of visualized music in Walt Disney's production *Fantasia*, thereby widening the

*Opposite*: Mickey as "The Sorcerer's Apprentice."

Reviewing storyboards for the "Rite of Spring" sequence are (left to right) Deems Taylor, Walt, and Stokowski.

Walt with Stravinsky

*Opposite:* Beethoven's "Pastoral Symphony."

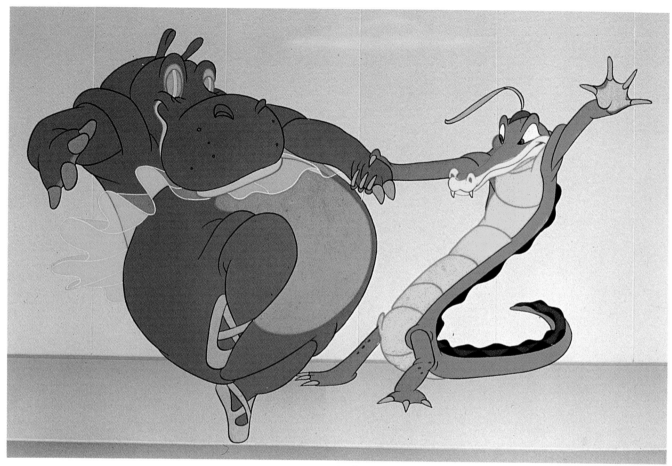

An "unusual" ballet from Ponchielli's "Dance of the Hours."

scope of the motion picture as entertainment and as an art form." Also, in 1941, the Academy presented Walt with the prestigious Irving Thalberg Memorial Award "for consistent high quality productions."

Fantasound was unlike any previous sound system. It used multiple speakers strategically placed throughout the theater and two projectors—one for the film and the other for the sound. It also was the first time that multiple sound tracks were used for recording and playback.

During the recording session, with Stokowski conducting his Philadelphia Orchestra, nine groups of microphones were located throughout the orchestra. Each was connected through the usual amplifying equipment to individual sound-on-film recorders. Each recorder took care of a specific part of the orchestra such as woodwinds, strings, and percussion. This made it possible to record the tonal quality of each section rather than using one sound track to capture the entire orchestra and losing the

more delicate passages of music.

When the recording was completed, the nine sound tracks went to Disney for mixing, using a process that today would be considered primitive. Each of the nine tracks were put on playback units, which were connected through three variable controls to amplifiers and other recorders. Using the variable controls, the sound engineers could vary the volume from a particular section of the orchestra and, at the same time, determine the speaker location or position from which the sound would emanate during the showing of the film. Through this process the nine original sound tracks were merged into three tracks.

With conventional sound film, a narrow strip located between the edge of the picture and the film perforation carries the film's sound track. With the Fantasound system, there are two separate reels of film. One reel is similar to conventional film, containing the picture and the complete sound track (used for backup only on *Fantasia*). The second reel contains four individual sound tracks; three tracks carry the recorded music, and sound and feed, respectively, the speakers located on the left, center and right of the theater, and the fourth track controls the volume and the position of the sound. The two projectors used for the showing are precisely synchronized so that picture and sound matching are flawless.

For the film's premiere, the Fantasound system used 90 speakers. Thirty-six were positioned backstage, with the rest located throughout the orchestra and balcony sections of the theater. The result was that the sound and music enveloped the audience and followed the movement of the screen action with uncanny fidelity.

Fantasia premiered in New York at the Broadway Theater (the former Colony Theater where Mickey Mouse made his debut) and was critically acclaimed for the the most part, with music purists being in the minority. In *Theatre Arts*, Isaacs called it: "an ingenious partnership between fine music and

animated film." *Time* magazine devoted a cover story to it. In an accompanying interview, Disney commented that he expected *Fantasia* to run for years, "perhaps even after I am gone." Otis Ferguson, in *The New Republic*, commented: "Fantasia is the only excuse I have ever seen for having ears and eyes at the same time." Philip T. Hartung, in *Commonweal*, commented: "Fantasia is a rare treat . . . to Walt Disney should go fresh laurels for giving us a new artistic experience of great beauty— another milestone in the motion picture." Some critics took exception to specific sequences in the film, but the general consensus was that Walt Disney had truly outdone himself.

In a review in *McCall's* magazine, Pare Lorentz commented: "I advise you to disregard the howls from the music critics; *Fantasia* is a Disney and not a classical conception of a concert, and even though the music is broader and more powerful than any you've heard from the screen, it is the imagery, and

Stokowski conducting a mock orchestra on a Disney Studio sound stage.

not the scores you will follow during the show. Thus, you can dismiss the complaints of the little hierarchy of music men who try to make music a sacrosanct, mysterious, and obscure art. Disney has brought it out of the temple, put it in carpet slippers and an old sweater, and made it work to surround, and support, and synchronize a brilliantly-drawn series of animated color sketches.''

Even before *Fantasia* was released, Walt and Stokowski were planning a sequel—another concert feature. Among the music that was considered was the overture to Rossini's *Barber of Seville*, Mozart's *Marriage of Figaro*, Dvorak's "New World Symphony," and Prokofiev's *Peter and the Wolf*. Only the last eventually made it to the screen.

Walt's original idea was to equip select theaters across the country with Fantasound and release *Fantasia* on a city-by-city basis as the systems were installed. Unfortunately, war production requirements curtailed RCA's ability to supply speakers, and the film was not widely released, which led to its commercial failure. Finally, in an attempt to recoup some of the production costs, Disney cut the length of the film and released it using the standard film soundtrack. In 1942, 43 minutes of the film were deleted, including the entire Bach segment. In 1956, the film was restored to approximately its original length and released in stereo using a four-track magnetic format.

It was not until the Seventies that *Fantasia* achieved new popularity. Among the teen and post-teen generation of that era, the "psychedelic" nature of the visuals produced a new wave of interest in the film.

More than forty years after *Fantasia*'s release, the Disney studio, recognizing the continuing popularity of the film and the deteriorating soundtrack, decided to re-record the score. Rather than take the traditional approach, the studio followed the Disney tradition of experimentation and used digital sound recording and playback for the film—still another first for the studio, and a reminder that Disney's pioneering spirit was still alive.

The process of re-recording the score for *Fantasia* was not an easy one. With the original, the music was recorded first, with the animation drawn to synchronize with the music. Now, the music had to be recorded to synchronize with the animation. Adding to the difficulties was the fact that some scenes in Beethoven's "Pastoral Symphony" had been deleted from the film, and Stokowski had taken some generous artistic liberties with the original scores.

Chosen to handle the project was Irwin Kostal, who was no stranger to Disney, film music, or classical music. Kostal had won two Oscars for his arrangements and orchestrations for *West Side Story* and *The Sound of Music*. For Disney, he handled the scores and orchestrations for *Mary Poppins*, *Bedknobs and Broomsticks*, and *Pete's Dragon*. During his early training, he studied classical music under the direction of the highly respected composer-conductor Nikolai Malko.

Kostal spent more than three months immersed in *Fantasia*'s original orchestral scores to better understand what Stokowski was trying to accomplish with his interpretations of the music. Larry Blake, in an article in *Recording Engineer/Producer*, notes: "One of the more unique problems was faced with Beethoven's *Sixth Symphony*. In the original version of the film, there was a scene where black centaurs could be seen shining the hooves of the white centaurs. It was not until the Sixties that this scene was regarded as offensive, and at that point deleted; the accompanying music was also removed, resulting in an abrupt cut. This 'across the board' cut of the music was done for the sake of convenience, since everything before and after the cut would remain in its original sync.

"For this reason, and because of cuts made by Stokowski himself, Kostal prepared 50 versions of the first two minutes of the Beethoven segment: 'I worked very hard to stick with the original Beethoven as much as I could. It was really difficult, because to preserve the order of the beginning meant that, in our version of *Fantasia*, all the music of approximately the first minute and 45 seconds was different than Stokowski. The reason for this was that the cuts were so bad. Some of this had to do with his cuts, but most of it was terrible things, like the across the board cuts, and cuts which removed the downbeat or the upbeat. It was ruined.'"

After he had solved these problems, Kostal hand-picked 127 musicians from the Los Angeles area, including five who had worked on the original

Irwin Kostal handled the re-recording of the *Fantasia* score in 1982.

recording. Instead of listening to his own orchestra during the recording session, Kostal listened through his earphones to Stokowski's original score and the click-track to better emulate the original.

The re-recording of *Fantasia* represented the first time that digital sound recording was used for a motion picture score. Digital recording is a technique that in effect measures sound, converting these measurements into a series of numbers that are stored on tape. As an example, during the digital recording of *Fantasia*, the audio signal was converted into the form of 50,000 different numbers every second. These numbers are then reconverted into accurate reproductions of the original measurements by a computer which generates a standard audio signal. The advantages to digital recording are that the technique is immune to error and distortion, and as many copies as needed can be made from the digital original with virtually no loss in quality.

Once the re-recording was complete, Disney engineers, led by Dave Brand, developed a proprietary projection system that utilized that digital track. In conventional projection systems, the soundtrack is synchronized with the film using the sprocket holes. With the digital process, time coding or "electronic sprocket holes" are used. Brand and his crew developed the interfaces and controls that enabled the projector to accurately "read" the track so that it was synchronized with the picture.

In 1982, the digital soundtrack version of *Fantasia* had its debut in Los Angeles at the Plitt Theater in Century City. According to Myron Meisel in *Film Journal*: "The technological quality of theater sound achieved a significant advance closer to that of original sound recording . . . .Fantasia happened to be a particularly felicitous test case, because its track is continuous orchestral music, so that the experience could be easily compared with the live experience of such sounds in a concert hall . . . the quiet passages in particular sound pristine. The clarity and crispness were virtually without discernible distortion, nor was there any audible noise . . . ."

Although Disney would go on to conquer many other new frontiers in the art of film and music, *Fantasia* may have represented a certain high point in his creative quest that even he felt would be difficult to surpass. "I can never build another *Fantasia*," he was reported to have said when the film was released. "I can improve. I can elaborate. That's all."

# CHAPTER FIVE

## *New Horizons in Film Music*

From the inception of *Snow White* through the release of *Bambi* in 1942, Walt Disney embarked on a journey that resulted in major advances in animation and in the integration of music with film. He went far beyond what other film makers were doing and, in the process, established new standards by which other animated films, and other Disney films, would be judged.

Each of the five animated films produced during this era, *Snow White, Pinocchio, Fantasia, Dumbo,* and *Bambi,* made significant contributions to the art of animation and film music. And, each in its own way, was an experiment that proved successful.

# Pinocchio

*Pinocchio* followed closely on the heels of *Snow White*, released three years later in 1940. Like *Snow White*, it also had what one reviewer called an "Old World operetta ambiance and storybook charm." *Pinocchio* demonstrated that Disney was the unchallenged master of the animated film. As children's author/illustrator Maurice Sendak commented in the *Los Angeles Times* on the film's re-release in 1978: "Pinocchio is Disney's masterpiece and, in my opinion, the most beautifully crafted of all animated films." Sendak continued: "The most significant feature, for me, is the musical score. A number of reviewers compared the songs unfavorably to the more tuneful *Snow White* music. What they failed to realize is that the score is a vital, integral part of the whole; nothing was allowed to obtrude even at the risk of sacrificing obvious melody and the hit song charts."

The immortal classic, "When You Wish Upon A Star," made its debut in *Pinocchio*. It was to become virtually *the* Disney theme song. Beginning in the Fifties, it was used as the opening for the Disney television show, *Disneyland*, and more than any other song since, is synonymous with Disney. It was also the first Disney song to win an Oscar (two later songs, "Zip-A-Dee-Doo-Dah" and "Chim Chim Cher-ee," also were honored with Oscars). Written by Leigh Harline with lyrics by Ned Washington, the song epitomizes the irresistible charm of the Disney movies. Sung by Jiminy Cricket (the voice of Cliff Edwards), the song opens the film:

*When you wish upon a star,*
*makes no diff'rence who you are,*
*Anything your heart desires will come to you.*

*If your heart is in your dreams*
*No request is too extreme,*
*When you wish upon a star,*
*As dreamers do.*

*Fate is kind,*
*she brings to those who love,*
*The sweet fulfillment of their secret longing.*
*Like a bolt out of the blue,*
*fate steps in and sees you thru,*
*When you wish upon a star your dreams come true.*

There are many aspects of *Pinocchio* that make it unique. It was the first Disney feature-length film to extensively use the multi-plane camera, which put *Pinocchio* on an entirely new visual level. The colors are lush and the camera produces a life-like, three-dimensional visual experience.

The musical score was equally lush and was also honored with an Oscar (the other Disney scores to receive Oscars were *Dumbo* and *Mary Poppins*). Leigh Harline was most responsible for the songs and the score. In one writer's judgment, Harline's work represented the longest individual musical contribution made by a single composer to any Disney animated feature.

Although Harline made the largest contribution to the film, several others were involved with the creation of the music, and *Pinocchio's* score is an example of close collaboration required to produce a film score. Paul Smith was involved in the composition and development of the score, and Ed Plumb, Frederick Stark, and Charles Wolcott were responsible for the orchestration. As Hollywood music critic Vernon Steele noted: "The manner in which these men worked together is of interest because it is an example of the sort of cooperation that makes for a well-rounded score. As in all other pictures, the several character themes, or leitmotifs, are employed in various ways according to the sequences under which they lie. As an example, the Jiminy Cricket theme, as it is first heard, is a joyous, tripping sort of thing, but in the course of the picture it is used to indicate nearly every motion. The three men who did nearly all of the orchestration, naturally, have varying abilities in handling rhythmic figures while another may find it easier or more agreeable—therefore more effective—to orchestrate romantic, dramatic or tragic sequences. So, as the Jiminy Cricket theme reappeared in varying form, it was orchestrated by the man who found the immediate task to his liking and proficiency. This of course resulted in getting the best possible work from each of the orchestrators and, naturally, better and more varied orchestrations than might otherwise have been the case."

Pinocchio begins in a world of song and dance, but becomes increasingly songless as the narrative moves closer and closer to the purely natural world.

Jiminy Cricket, the narrator of *Pinocchio*, opens the
film by singing the immortal classic "When You Wish
Upon A Star."

Even without songs in the later segments of the film, it is beautifully scored and never loses the feeling of a full-scale musical.

After Jiminy Cricket opens the film singing "When You Wish Upon A Star," he admonishes the audience "I'll bet a lot of you folks don't believe that." He confesses he didn't either, until a startling experience changed his mind. He then opens the storybook and begins to narrate the tale of Pinocchio.

The scene shifts to the shop of Geppetto the woodcarver, who is putting the finishing touches on a marionette—Pinocchio. As Geppetto sleeps, the Blue Fairy appears and gives Pinocchio life, although he still remains wooden. The Blue Fairy appoints Jiminy Cricket as Pinocchio's official conscience.

What follows is a series of adventures for Pinocchio and Jiminy. In adapting Collodi's nineteenth-century children's novel, the Disney writers faced the problem of continuity and drama, since the original was in the form of more than forty serialized chapters. In Pinocchio's first misadventure, he is lured by the sly fox, Honest John, to join Stromboli's puppet show. On the way to Stromboli's, Pinocchio sings the bouncy "Hi-Diddle-Dee-Dee (An Actor's Life For Me)." Then, during the puppet show, he sings and dances to "I've Got No Strings," a simple tune that celebrates Pinocchio's freedom:

> I've got no strings to hold me down,
> To make me fret, or make me frown,
> I had strings but now I'm free,
> There are no strings on me.
> Hi-o the merrio,
> That's the only way to be.
> I want the world to know nothing ever worries me,
> I've got no strings so I have fun,
> I'm not tied up to anyone,
> They've got strings, but you can see
> There are no strings on me.

The Blue Fairy rescues Pinocchio, but not before he tells the lies that cause his nose to grow. In the next sequence, Pinocchio ventures off to Pleasure Island where naughty little boys are turned into jackasses. After escaping, he returns home to find that Geppetto has been swallowed by the whale,

Pinocchio's "official conscience."

Monstro. He goes after Geppetto and rescues him from the belly of the whale. Pinocchio dies during the rescue, but the Blue Fairy enters the scene and gives him life as a real live boy. At this point, Jiminy leaves with the comment that this is where he came in, and we hear a reprise of "When You Wish Upon A Star."

As the mood and the action of the film move from the happiness of Geppetto's workshop to the terror of the whale, the music shifts dramatically. Fewer and fewer songs are heard as the characters experience more and more terrifying situations. The background score, moved with this change in emphasis. As Paul Smith, who contributed to the background score explained, "The old-world quality of Geppetto's life was caught by the tinkle of the music boxes. The quaintness of the village was tonally fixed by the themes of set, long-ago rhythms. The whale and the fishing scenes were scored in distinctly modern tonality, to suggest eeriness."

Even the sound effects used in the film were musical in nature which, in fact, was not unusual for a Disney film. In many instances, the sound-effects men, many of whom were musicians, turned to musical instruments for their inspiration for new sounds. For example, to achieve the music box sounds in *Pinocchio*, it would have been simple to use an actual music box. However, to create the most "musical" music box, an orchestra was used, performing in such a way as to produce the "mechanical" sounds of a music box.

The musical score was an important element in giving *Pinocchio* its cohesiveness. Leonard Maltin, who chronicled the studio's productions in *The Disney Films*, commented: "The musical score was one of the finest (written) for Disney, not only supplementing the action but playing a major role in creating the desired moods." Throughout the film, subtle musical themes are used as leitmotifs to support characters and situations within the film. For example, there is a hippity-hop rhythm identified with Jiminy Cricket. Every time that Jiminy is about to be the center of action, the rhythm is subtly contained in the background music. Whenever Jiminy and the Blue Fairy get together to help Pinocchio, some variation of "When You Wish Upon A Star" is heard.

At the end of the film, with Jiminy leading the way back to Geppetto's house, the house is exaggeratedly empty until Jiminy seems to take over and all is well. Smith explained how music was used to help build the various moods. At first, there is the hopping theme. As they get closer to the house, Geppetto's theme, "Little Wooden Head," is heard. The emptiness of the house is symbolized by an uplifting sound when Jiminy appears in the window. Smith said: "The entire sequence is good cartoon music, skipping, with exaggerated relief, to character suggestion, to action, all in the space of a few minutes, and covering a wide range of feeling in a way that is musical despite its exaggeration."

Although *Pinocchio* was an instant critical success, it was not a commercial one. With the war raging in Europe, these markets were now closed to Disney. It was not until the film was re-released after the war that the studio recouped its investment in the film. In 1985, the film was released on video cassette for enjoyment by an even larger audience.

# Dumbo

Dumbo, released in 1941, is the one of the shortest Disney animated features, just over one hour in length, and it is pure Disney. It has a simple story about a lovable baby elephant who, ridiculed because of his big ears, accidentally discovers he can fly. And, its circus setting provides the color, music, and excitement that the child in everyone can relate to.

As Ward Kimball, who worked on the animation of *Dumbo*, commented: "Sure, we've done things that have had a lot more finish, frosting, and tricky footwork, but basically, I think the Disney cartoon reached its zenith with *Dumbo*. To me, it is the one feature cartoon that has a foolproof plot. Every story element meshes into place, held together with the great fantasy of a flying elephant. The first time I heard Walt outline the plot I knew that the picture had great simplicity and cartoon heart."

Frank Churchill and Ned Washington teamed up to do the songs. Although no major hits emerged from the film, the nine songs used are skillfully blended into the story to give it the feel of a pure musical. The uptempo music conveys the sights and sounds of circus life, such as the "Song of the Roustabouts" while the circus tent is being set up, and the bright, brassy "It's Circus Day Again" as the musical setting for a colorful circus parade.

As the film opens, babies are being delivered to animal members of the circus, except for one elephant, Mrs. Jumbo, whose stork is late. According to Dick Huemer, who was involved with developing the story, "It was suggested in a story meeting that we would show the stork with the baby looking for Mrs. Jumbo to deliver it to, and we thought, 'Why not have a song to set up the stork on his mission.' So Ned Washington came up with 'Look out for Mr. Stork . . . that funny little chap . . . he'll come along and drop . . . a baby in your lap,' and so forth. All his own lyrics. A lyric that is sometimes atmospheric. It gives you a comic slant on the stork and his business, and also the rather important story point- the happily anticipated arrival of Dumbo."

Shortly after Dumbo arrives at the circus, it's discovered that he has huge ears for an elephant—long enough so that he stumbles over them when walking. The other elephants express horror, sarcasm and disdain, and poor, little Dumbo is treated as an outcast. Later, Dumbo gets into trouble as a clown in the circus and Mrs. Jumbo, while trying to protect her baby, is locked up as a wild elephant. When Dumbo comes to visit her, she sings the touching song "Baby Mine," which was nominated for an Academy Award:

*Baby mine don't you cry*
*Baby mine dry your eye*
*Rest your head close to my heart,*
*Never to part, Baby of mine.*

*Little one when you play*
*Don't you mind what they say*
*Let those eyes sparkle and shine,*
*Never a tear, Baby of mine.*

*From your head to your toes*
*You're so sweet, goodness knows*
*You're so precious to me*
*Cute as can be, Baby of mine.*

After getting into trouble, Dumbo discovers a much-needed friend in Timothy, a sassy little mouse. During one of the most imaginative sequences of the film, Dumbo is cast as a clown in the circus, and he unknowingly drinks from a bucket of water into which a bottle of champagne has fallen. What follows is one of the most delightful sequences of the film, "Pink Elephants On Parade." In this sequence, Dumbo is challenged by Timothy to blow different types of bubbles, and one of the bubbles becomes a pink elephant. The "bubble" elephant blows another bubble out of his trunk, and soon there are four elephants using their trunks to herald the song "Pink Elephants On Parade." What follows is a surreal fantasy of design, space, color, light, and gags. The song "Pink Elephants," with words by Ned Washington and music by Oliver Wallace, was set to a minor key march, and the song's lyrics convey the feel of the nightmare Dumbo is experiencing:

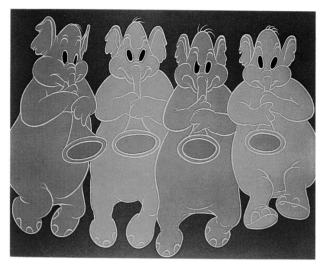

"Pink Elephants on Parade."

*Look out! Look out!*
*Pink elephants on parade,*
*Here they come!*
*Hippety hoppety, they're here and there,*
*Pink Elephants everywhere.*

*Look out! Look out!*
*They're walking around the bed,*
*on their heads,*
*Clippety cloppety, arrayed in braid,*
*Pink elephants on parade.*

*What'll I do?*
*What'll I do?*
*What an unusual view!*

*I can stand the sight of worms,*
*and look at microscopic germs,*
*But Technicolor pachyderms is really too much*
*for me.*

*I am not the type to faint when things are odd,*
*or things are quaint,*
*But seeing things you know that ain't*
*can certainly give you an awful fright.*

*What a sight!*
*Chase 'em away!*
*Chase 'em away!*
*I'm afraid, need your aid,*
*Pink elephants on parade!*
*Pink elephants!*

Leonard Maltin commented on this: "There is no way to overpraise the 'Pink Elephants' scene. It is one of the best things ever done at the Disney studio, and, to use a much overworked but appropriate phrase, years ahead of its time."

Following this sequence, Dumbo awakens to find himself and Timothy up in a tree surrounded by black crows who proceed to try and convince Dumbo that he *flew* up into the tree. Ross Care, in his profile on Ward Kimball, notes: "It was the 'When I See An Elephant Fly/Black Crow' sequence in *Dumbo* that really gave Kimball his first chance to 'solo' and merge his unique flair for the musical set-piece with an equally distinctive style of vigorous, rhythmic, character animation. In this visual episode, the characterizations grow out of the musical material itself, or more accurately, the song and the characterizations evolve in a parallel manner, each element felicitously interlocking in a free-wheeling but precisely choreographed synthesis."

Kimball commented on the sequence: "It evolved from the fact that it was a crucial story point, where the birds had to convince the mouse, Timothy, and Dumbo that they could not have gotten up in the tree by any other means but by flying. Of course, this was vital to the plot, and Walt saw the chance to do a big musical number. I think a lot of the development and gags were achieved on the night we recorded the song. Cliff Edwards doing the voice of Jim Crow really made the whole sequence, because he was quite adept at doing kazoo solos on his old records, and he could vocally imitate other instruments. Many of the instrumental effects on the track were done by Edwards: voice-wise, he really sounded more black than the blacks we had backing him up.

"The voices we used for the other crows were from the Hall Johnson Choir, a group from a well-known black church in Los Angeles. That's why the development and differentiation of the characters really began on the night that we started recording. After listening to the voices, I decided that maybe the squeaky, high voice might be the little crow with the kid's cap and pink glasses, and Jim Crow would be the big, dominating boss crow with the derby. Later, I began to graphically re-design the characters to make them emphatically different types. This took place in a lot of pictures we worked on; in the beginning you'd

"When I See An Elephant Fly."

only have a miscellaneous set of characters, but by the time the voices were set, you have a pretty good idea how they would individually look, react, and even function in the sequence."

The song "When I See An Elephant Fly" was designed to give the crows a vehicle to poke fun of Dumbo without being nasty. The lyrics are a delightful collection of puns:

*I seen a peanut stand,*
*and heard a rubber band,*
*I seen a needle that winked its eye,*
*But I be done seen about everything*
*when I see an elephant fly.*

*I've seen a front porch swing,*
*heard a diamond ring,*
*I seen a polka dot railroad tie,*
*But I be done seen about everything*
*when I see an elephant fly.*

At the happy conclusion of the film, Dumbo has become an international celebrity, and his mother now rides in her own streamlined railroad car on the circus train.

In recalling Walt Disney's involvement with the songs in his films, Dick Huemer stated: "That feeling is written in there of a musical nightmare. Ned Washington wrote the lyrics, and he would be in on the story meetings and would present his songs, he'd tap them out with his fingers. Walt didn't have quite the grasp of music that he had of other things. That was one place where he was somewhat at the mercy of his musicians and lyric writers. If there was a poor lyric, he couldn't say, 'Well, why don't we say so-and-so,' because he wasn't a great poet or at least a rhymester, which it takes to be a lyricist, I guess. Nevertheless, I understand it was he who came up with the line: 'It's a Zip-A-Dee-Doo-Dah day,' which became a hit in *Song of the South*. But generally he just okayed (or didn't okay) a lyric or melody. A songwriter would mostly put his own work through just about the way he had written it. But he had to make it fit, which could always be done, of course. I've done that sort of thing myself, on occasion. For instance, we would say, 'Let's write a song . . . a mother song for when she's chained up and Dumbo comes to visit her.' Well, naturally, there's some heartbreaking type of lyric indicated, and in this case Ned Washington came up with 'Baby mine, don't you cry . . .' A heartbreaker."

*Dumbo* received excellent reviews, and the film's musical score by Oliver Wallace and Frank Churchill won the Academy Award for best musical score. *Newsweek* commented: "Those Walt Disney fans who feared the worst when the Master went 'arty' with *Fantasia*, then missed the boat with the experimental *The Reluctant Dragon**, can now un-cross their fingers, sit back and relax. Dumbo's in town."

Reviewer Cecilia Ager commented in *PM*: "*Dumbo* is the nicest, kindest Disney yet. It has the most heart, taste, beauty, compassion, skill, restraint. It marks a return to Disney's first principles, the animal kingdom—that happy land where Disney workers turn into artists; where their imagination, playfulness, ingenuity, daring flourish freest;

---

* *The Reluctant Dragon* (1941) was Disney's first major use of live-action combined with animation in a feature-length film. It starred Robert Benchley, and included a tour of the Disney studio.

where, in short, they're home. *Dumbo*'s the most enchanting and endearing of their output, maybe because it's the least pretentious of their works, the least self-conscious. It tries only to be a wonderful example of a form they themselves created—the fable expressing universal human truths in animal guise.''

# Bambi

*Bambi* is the antithesis of *Dumbo*. While *Dumbo* was bright and brassy, *Bambi* is soft and gentle. The film is almost devoid of dialogue, with only about nine hundred words used in the entire film. Music takes the place of the spoken word.

*Bambi* was initiated in 1937 after Walt read the Felix Salten book and decided it was the type of project he wanted to do. The film took five years to produce, which was longer than most of Disney's films up to this point. This delay was due in part to the other films in production at the time, but it was Walt's meticulous attention to detail that caused the most delays. For example, he had live animals brought into the studio to be studied and sketched so that the animators would be able to reflect in their drawings the fluid motion of the animals. A film crew was sent to Maine to study and photograph the animals in their natural habitat. Even the songs were animated with minute attention to detail, as in the song ''Little April Shower,'' where the introduction shows close-ups of individual raindrops falling and splattering, with woodwinds providing the sound effects.

*Bambi* musically bridges the gap between those films that rely on music only for background mood, and those musical films in which scenes and action are built around a hit song. In *Bambi*, the action flows with the music. The songs, by Frank Churchill and Larry Morey, are sung by a forty-voice chorus. The film's opening song, ''Love Is A Song,'' is heard throughout the background score. The song and score were both nominated for Academy Awards.

Ross B. Care, in his study ''Threads of Melody: The Evolution of a Major Film Score—Walt Disney's *Bambi*,'' comments: ''Disney wished to render this story visually and musically, and it is in *Bambi*'s background score that the sound track reaches its apex of classical beauty. As in *Dumbo*, the score shuns *Snow White*'s operetta structure with its aria-like vocal solos and lively production numbers, opting instead for a subtext which weaves songs and incidental music cunningly together to the virtual exclusion of the solo. The resulting construct is a seamless musical tapestry which envelops the tenuously plotted story in a delirious, lyrical haze of piquant melodies and complexly modernistic, programmatic background scoring.

''The Greek chorus of the sawdust which supported *Dumbo*'s diverse happenings becomes, in *Bambi*, the veritable voice of nature. At times heard *en masse*, at others fragmented into separate sections or even soloists (the latter employed impressionistically and not for purposes of individual showcasing), the choral voices project both song lyrics ('Little April Shower' and 'I Bring You A Song') and the purely phonetic sounds (similar in effect to the mythic, pantheistic, orchestral-choral textures of Ravel's *Daphnis and Chloe* and Ralph Vaughan Williams' *Flos Campi*) heard during the opening multiplane pan, the autumn and winter montages, and at various points throughout the film.''

Based on Salten's book, *Bambi* simply presents the cycle of life in the forest. It opens with the birth of Bambi and follows him through the seasons as he grows and experiences the many delights found in the tranquillity of the forest. But man enters and death follows. However, even after a devastating man-caused forest fire, life continues. Bambi woos the beautiful Faline, sires two off-spring, and matures to become the new prince of the forest. We are also introduced to two delightful new Disney characters in the film, Thumper the rabbit and Flower the skunk.

Walt Disney was emphatic about the role music would play in *Bambi*. At a story conference in 1940, he told the story director, Perce Pearce, ''You have to have a powerful music score on this. I tell you it will add to the picture's greatness if you do have a marvelous musical score, one that expresses the action and gives focus to it. How many words of dialogue have we got in this picture?'' Pearce responded: ''900. There ought to be 875.'' Walt said: ''You see how important music is?''

Walt had live animals brought into the studio to be studied so that the animators would be able to reflect in their drawings the fluid motion of the animals.

In another story conference, Walt stated: "We've got to take this thing and make it appeal to a very broad audience. The music has to give dramatic emphasis, and I feel a monotony to it." One of the sequence directors, James Algar, asked: "Would you see more definite synching of the music to the picture?" Walt replied: "I see a bit more guts to it, maybe even overdoing it. You might say on the corny side, in some spots, but with the old dramatic force of a good orchestra behind it. It think it's a risky thing and it's wrong for us to try to be too clever with our music. And, there's the risk of letting the picture down, you see. I'm for getting out of ruts, but I'm just a little worried about being too subtle or playing our music to those certain few who might think it's clever. The rest will be missing it from the dramatic side. Basically the music we will have is there now— and I don't know—it adds a certain monotony to me.

Wherever you can, get melody in the music and stress it. It would give the picture a lift, and you've got to do it with music."

At this point, Sam Armstrong, another sequence director, said: "It means thinking in terms of a bigger orchestra than was contemplated at first." Walt replied: "No, in terms of more showmanship with the music. The music has to supply something that would ordinarily be supplied with dialogue and a more gripping story maybe. The music has to supply that, and it can. I think at times you have to use 40 or 50 pieces for your peak dramatic points. There's a lot of places where a smaller orchestra, even down to the point of five instruments for some of the cuter, lighter stuff, will serve."

The background score for *Bambi* was primarily composed by Frank Churchill. Edward Plumb was also involved in some notable sequences, including the fire scene. Plumb had studied under Johann Strauss and had been an arranger for Paul Whiteman and Andre Kostelanetz, to name only two. Paul Smith did much of the orchestration of the background score and it was a rich experience for him. He later recalled: "For some reason, I found animal and nature films a joy to work on. This was especially true with the True-Life series. Even though, as a child, I had no pets. I think it provided an opportunity and setting for me to use my classical training in new and imaginative ways." Also working on the orchestration was Charles Wolcott, who joined the studio in 1938 after a career in New York that included arranging for the Paul Whiteman Orchestra and Bob Hope's radio show.

There are many musical and visual highlights in the film. In the "winter" sequence, Bambi and Thumper come face to face with snow and ice for the first time, and they try to maneuver on the ice of a frozen pond to the background sounds of a skater's waltz. Another delightful moment occurs when

Thumper falls victim to "twitterpation," a Disney euphemism for sexual awakening and love. Ross Care commented that the accompanying background music for this sequence demonstrated a good example of theme and variations. He wrote: "As each character experiences the various manifestations of love (from the ridiculous to the sublime), Churchill's basic musical theme, first heard at the beginning of the sequence as Friend Owl explains Twitterpation, underscores each encounter with an appropriate musical transformation—from waltz to march to a lewdly screaming solo clarinet variation."

Care also commented on Plumb's scoring of the "Forest Fire" scene. He wrote: ". . . here the balance between music and visuals maintained throughout the film is somewhat stacked on the side of music. Though the fire sequence generates moments of great impact, its visuals cannot always match the crackling momentum of Plumb's brilliant scoring. Though the music-visual balance is re-established in the fire's climactic shots (which include an awesome aerial multiplane pan as the Great Stag and Bambi leap to safety over the brink of a huge waterfall), the fire sequence as a whole would, one suspects, be greatly diminished in impact if deprived of its acutely augmenting musical underlay."

Frank Churchill (at the piano) and Larry Morey collaborated on the words and music to the songs from *Bambi*.

Edward Plumb composed the background score for the forest fire scene.

# CHAPTER SIX

## *The South American Adventure*

**W**ith America's entry into World War II, the Disney studio soon focused over 90 percent of its efforts on war-related projects. For example, Walt Disney's animators and artists designed insignia for the Allied forces. Soon, the images of Pluto, Donald, and a variety of other Disney characters appeared on jeeps, trucks, tanks, and aircraft. Walt also produced a variety of film projects for the war effort. He made training films for the Army and the Navy; and, the studio produced a number of educational films for the National Film Board of Canada, the Department of Agriculture, the Treasury Department, and the State Department, with such titles as *Food Will Win the War, Four Methods of Flush Riveting, Stop that Tank,* and *Out of the Frying Pan into the Firing Line.* It was estimated that Disney turned out more than 300,000 feet of film for the government.

The studio suffered financially from its war efforts. Although there were opportunities to profit from government contracts, Walt was more concerned with contributing to the overall war effort. As he explained in a 1942 interview: "It's hard to say good things about a war, but this is a tremendous opportunity to show what our medium can do. The hell with the six percent we could have made on our government work. Not many people have a chance like this to help both their country and themselves."

Several propaganda films produced by Disney during the war enjoyed success. One was a full-length feature entitled *Victory through Air Power* that combined animation and live action. Using animation, Disney traced the history and development of aviation. This propaganda film aimed at increasing America's air power. The film's director, H. C. Potter, recalled in an interview: "The British Air Force thought this was the greatest thing that ever came down the pike, and the picture was much better known in England than it was here, in official circles, and early in the game. Walt told me this story, and swore this was what happened. When Churchill came over to the Quebec conference, they were trying to get Roosevelt interested in this long-range bombing idea, and Roosevelt didn't know what the hell they were talking about. Churchill said, 'Well, of course, you've seen *Victory through Air Power . . . ,*' and Roosevelt said, 'No, what's that?' Air Marshall Tedder and Churchill worked on Roosevelt until Roosevelt put out an order to the Air Corps to fly a print of *Victory through Air Power* up to Quebec. Churchill ran it for him, and that was the beginning of the U.S. Air Corps Long Range Bombing."

Although no original songs were written for *Victory through Air Power*, the film's score, written by Edward Plumb, Paul Smith, and Oliver Wallace, was nominated for an Academy Award.

Another film that proved to be extremely popular was a cartoon originally intended to be titled *Donald Duck in Nutzi Land* that featured an Oliver Wallace song, "Der Fuehrer's Face." This was a raucous ditty, complete with Bronx cheers, that gave Donald an opportunity to release his volatile temper against Hitler. It also gave a war-weary public a rallying point.

According to studio records, the song was published before the film was released. Spike Jones, a trombonist in the John Scott Trotter band and the leader of his own jazz group called The City Slickers, decided to record it. It was used on the flip side of "I Wanna Go Back to West Virginia," which was supposed to be the main song on the record. When the record was released, however, it was "Der Fuehrer's Face" that drove sales over a million and a half copies and helped launch Spike Jones and The City Slickers as an entertainment phenomenon. Oscar Hammerstein II called it, "the great psychological song of the war." Before the cartoon was released in 1943, its title was changed to that of the song, and the film won an Oscar for that year's best animated short subject.

An equally important contribution that Disney made during these years was in the two films he produced following a trip to South America—*Saludos Amigos* and *The Three Caballeros*. In 1940, the U.S. State Department had established the Office of the Coordinator of Inter-American Affairs with Nelson Rockefeller in charge. The next year, Rockefeller and John Hay (Jock) Whitney, who was in charge of the Motion Picture Section, approached Walt with a proposal to make a tour of South America and make some films as part of the Good Neighbor policy.

The timing for such a trip was right. The war had closed many European distribution channels, and South America represented a new market for Disney films. In addition, there was a bitter strike taking place at the studio, and many studio executives felt it would be settled more quickly without Walt's personal involvement. So Disney packed a crew, including music director Charles Wolcott, and headed south of the border for several months. As a studio press release noted at the time, the purpose of the trip was "to utilize properly, in the medium of animation, some of the vast wealth of South American literature, music and customs which has never failed to fascinate them."

Wolcott, who would eventually be nominated for three Academy Awards for his musical work on the films developed out of this trip, recalled: "Up until that time, my only exposure to Latin music was the sound of Xavier Cugat. It was a revealing experience,

*Der Fuehrer's Face* featured an Oliver Wallace title song.

as we had the opportunity to explore the countryside and gain insight into the music of the people." He was also fascinated with the handcrafted native instruments and the sounds they produced. He said, "One day I heard a haunting melody. It was being produced by reed pipes. Each was made to fit the fingers of the individual player. This gave the notes an off-pitch sound that was intriguing. When we returned to the studio, I was finally able to approximate the sound by using recorders. We incorporated this sound into a sequence in which Donald Duck is in Bolivia."

In the early 1940s, German influence in Latin America was widespread and German propaganda films played to large audiences. To counter this Axis activity, Rockefeller's office began a massive program to supply South America with motion pictures about the Allied nations. While Walt was working on the feature films resulting from the trip, he agreed to produce a series of educational films as well. This initial contract called for five subjects on health and five on agriculture. In early 1943, the first of these shorts was ready for release. Because these films were directed toward audiences that would include many illiterates, a sound-track narration was used

rather than printed titles. Color was also used, since its appeal would outweigh the cost. And, the cartoon format was used rather than live action since it offered more control over the subject being visualized.

The first non-short film completed as a result of the trip was *South of the Border With Disney*, which was released in late 1942. This one-half hour film simply recorded the group's South American trip, and was more of a travelogue than an entertainment film.

The next film was *Saludos Amigos*. It combined live action with animation, a technique Disney first experimented with in a 1941 release with Robert Benchley entitled *The Reluctant Dragon*. The film opens with the Disney crew boarding a plane in Los Angeles and heading for Bolivia. Donald Duck stars in the first cartoon segment, "Lake Titicaca," in which he plays an irrepressible tourist. Included in this segment is live-action footage of the lake and the beautiful Bolivian countryside.

The crew then travels to Chile where the second cartoon segment is about a family of mail planes. The young plane, Pedro, must fly over the mountains from Santiago to Mendoza and runs into trouble on his return trip. The sequence is reminiscent of the

"Little Engine That Could" segment of *Dumbo* with Casey, Jr., the little railroad engine battling a steep hill. The film moves from Chile to Argentina where the third segment, "El Gaucho Goofy," features Goofy in a variety of comic escapades as a gaucho.

The final sequence of the film, "Aquarela do Brasil," introduced a major new Disney character—Joe Carioca, a Brazilian parrot. His voice was provided by Jose Oliveira, a Brazilian musician who had directed Carmen Miranda's orchestra for ten years. The live-action footage that separates the two sequences shows several members of the Disney group dancing and playing instruments. Everything seen in this footage—the musical instruments, dances, costumes, and architecture—is later seen in the cartoon. In the cartoon, Donald Duck meets up with Joe Carioca during Carnival time in Rio de Janeiro, and Joe then takes Donald on a whirlwind tour of South America.

Two songs, "Brazil" (or "Aquarela do Brasil") and "Tico, Tico," though not written exclusively for the film, were incorporated into the score of the final segment. Ary Barroso wrote "Brazil" in 1939 and Eddy Duchin introduced it to the United States, where it was made popular by both Xavier Cugat and Jimmy Dorsey's orchestra. *Saludos Amigos* was the first time "Brazil" was used in a motion picture, and the catchy popular song was used several more times in later Hollywood films.

*Saludos Amigos* became the first Hollywood film to premiere in all Latin American countries before opening in the United States. The record crowds it drew in South America forced the suspension of the usual practice of showing double features in some areas. *Collier's* reported that some overly enthusiastic audiences were "threatening to tear down the theater if they didn't repeat *Saludos Amigos*." The title song, written by Wolcott with lyrics by Ned Washington, was nominated for an Academy Award.

Although *Saludos Amigos* served as a blueprint for *The Three Caballeros*, Walt had no desire to simply duplicate the first film. It was decided that a unique combination of live action with animation would distinguish the film from previous Disney films. Up to this point, although several films had used both live action and animation, Disney had only made limited attempts to combine the two within the same frame (*Alice Comedies*, *Fantasia*, and *The Reluctant Dragon*). This is what Walt dreamed of doing in *The Three Caballeros*.

Combining live action and animation in color was a difficult operation, but Walt insisted on developing and perfecting this technique. Ken Anderson, an art supervisor on the film, recalled that Walt "was always attempting to get something new that would really boggle the mind. And so he was impatient of limitations and technical restrictions of any kind. He wanted freedom to do anything which improved the illusion of reality."

Music for the film was provided by Manuel Esperon, Ary Barroso and Agustin Lara, along with Charles Wolcott and Ray Gilbert of the Disney staff. In a studio publicity release, Lara, Esperon, and Barroso are described as the Jerome Kern, Cole Porter, and Vincent Youmans of South America. In addition to the Latin composers, Disney signed three Latin American actresses to co-star in the film, Dora Luz and Carmen Molina of Mexico, and Brazil's Aurora Miranda, Carmen's sister who had already gained popularity in the U.S.

In the film, Donald Duck is reunited with Joe Carioca and they are joined by a new character, Panchito, a Mexican charro rooster. Since the film used three characters, Ray Gilbert wrote appropriate lyrics for the trio in the song "The Three Caballeros," and this was eventually chosen as the title for the film as well.

The structure of *The Three Caballeros* is carefully worked out in a tripartite manner. The film stars three cartoon characters, has three live actresses, and is comprised of three parts. The first sequence features Donald as the only caballero present. He receives a birthday package in which there are three short cartoons. One tells the story of Pablo the Penguin who can't get used to his Antarctic home and sails for the South Seas on his ice floe. Another is about a strange bird, the Aracuan bird. The final short is about Little Gauchito who finds a flying burrito (donkey) and enters it in a race. At the end, Joe Carioca pops out of the birthday package.

Donald and Joe Carioca in *Saludos Amigos*.

Walt expanded and perfected the technique of combining animation with live action in *The Three Caballeros.*

*Opposite.* The original cover to the Decca Album.

In the second segment, called "Baia," live action is first combined with animation and we are introduced to Aurora Miranda. Donald joins Miranda and her musician friends on the screen. At the end of her song, "Os Quindins De Yaya," Miranda's dancing becomes so infectious that the lamp posts and buildings start to sway and samba with her.

The final segment, "La Pinata," moves us to Mexico where we are introduced to Panchito. It is comprised of a series of short episodes as Panchito's magic serape becomes a flying carpet for the trio. In one episode, Carmen Molina appears in Tehuantepec costume to dance a Zandunga. Her live-action dancing is combined with the animated figure of Donald, who holds hands with her and spins himself into multiple images which surround the attractive actress. At one point, several animated cactus plants appear and Molina, now in Chihuahua costume, comes forward to dance the jesusita, or Cactus March. Donald joins her and even the cacti dance, as well as play calliope pipes and transform into small, green, duck-shaped plants which march over poor Donald.

Of the sixteen songs that were used in the film, two became song hits — "You Belong to My Heart" by Agustin Lara and Ray Gilbert and "Baia" by Ary Barroso and Gilbert.

Ward Kimball, who worked on the animation of the title song, recalled in an interview in *Funnyworld*: "It's fun to look at today. Everything else I have done, I criticize, I say I should have done this or that, but on *Three Caballeros*, I had a lot of fun. When you see it now, it's kind of old hat, characters going out on the left and coming in from the right, with no hookups, sort of a magic animation." In discussing the film in his *The Disney Films*, Leonard Maltin notes: "The combination of live action and animation . . . was perfect. The synchronization of movement between the actors and the cartoon characters is right on target, and the illusion is such that you are willing to believe that Donald and the bathing beauties are really frolicking together, or that Donald is actually dancing with Aurora Miranda and her musicians. These processes were developed by Walt's long-time colleague Ub Iwerks, who continued to refine them right through the 1960s and *Mary Poppins*."

Bobby Driscoll (left) with James Baskett as Uncle
Remus in *Song of the South*.

# CHAPTER SEVEN

## *The Postwar Years*

With the exception of the South American films produced under the auspices of the U.S. government, Disney did not have any major productions underway when the war came to a close. The studio had totally concentrated on the war effort, with no time spent developing commercial films. It was not until 1950, with the release of *Cinderella*, that Disney completed a feature-length animated film telling a single story.

During the years following the war, the studio was anxious to release films, so Disney developed a technique for animated films that would later be employed with his television show. He took a series of non-related shorts and released them in feature-length format. With these films, Disney went outside the studio and used well-known stars and entertainers to increase the box office appeal. Another direction Disney took was the further development of live-action films combined with animation. Live action took less time to develop and was less expensive than animation. The first such films, *Song of the South* and *So Dear to My Heart*, significantly advanced the art of combining live action with animation.

# The Animated Films

*Make Mine Music* (1946) was Disney's first feature-length film following the war. Subtitled "A Musical Fantasy in Ten Parts," it consisted of ten unrelated musical short subjects. The star-studded cast included the voices and music of Nelson Eddy, Dinah Shore, Benny Goodman and his orchestra, the Andrews Sisters, Jerry Colonna, and Sterling Holloway, a voice Disney would use in many films. Charles Wolcott was the musical director on the film and was assisted by Ken Darby, Oliver Wallace, and Ed Plumb. Ray Gilbert wrote the lyrics for most of the ten songs used in the film.

There were a number of memorable sequences in this film. The opening segment featured a fast-paced cartoon built around the classic hillbilly feud told in the song "The Martins and the Coys," which was sung by the King's Men. The second segment had as its title song "Blue Bayou," written by Bobby Worth and Ray Gilbert and sung by Ken Darby, which enjoyed some success on recordings. The animation for this segment was originally done as the "Clair de Lune" sequence planned for *Fantasia* but later dropped from that film.

There are two segments that feature the music of Benny Goodman. The first, *A Jazz Interlude*, has as its song "All the Cats Join In," written by Alec Wilder, Ray Gilbert, and Eddie Sauter. The animation, starting with simple pencil strokes, maintains a looseness to it as it depicts bobby-soxers living it up at a corner malt shop. The second Goodman segment has as its title song "After You've Gone," a popular standard of the Twenties by Henry Creamer and Turner Leighton, and it features the Goodman quartet with Cozy Cole, Teddy Wilson, and Sid Weiss. The animation presents a surreal depiction of musical instruments in an abstract battle. Leonard Maltin commented that this segment ". . . is among the best surreal animation Disney ever did, buoyed by the sparkling sounds of the Goodman quartet. It moves very fast, its imagination unflagging in presenting the four humanized instruments on the lam in their nightmarish world. . . ."

One particularly melodious segment is "Johnny Fedora and Alice Blue Bonnet," written by Allie Wrubel and Ray Gilbert. The song is sung by the harmonious voices of the Andrews Sisters, and it tells a delightful story of two hats that fall in love and the events that lead up to their eventual union.

A number that was planned for the sequel to *Fantasia* is seen in *Make Mine Music*. Prokofiev's classic *Peter and the Wolf* is narrated by Sterling Holloway. Although the animation and action are done in the Disney tradition, many reviewers felt this segment fell flat. Leonard Maltin commented: ". . . there is an inherent problem with the piece; it was designed to be heard, not seen. The famous narration, keyed to special orchestration of the music, was intended to fascinate children by making them use their imaginations to visualize the story. Hence, any visual treatment destroys the essential meaning of the piece."

Two other notable segments include "Casey at the Bat" and *Opera Pathetique* starring Willie the singing whale. For "Casey at the Bat," Ray Gilbert, Ken Darby, and Eliot Daniel wrote a score and song, "Casey, the Pride of Them All," that set to music the popular poem of how the mighty slugger Casey struck out that terrible day in Mudville. The narration and singing was handled by popular comedian/entertainer Jerry Colonna.

In "The Whale Who Wanted to Sing at the Met," Nelson Eddy is the featured performer who provides all the voices for this musical comedy of Willie the whale who could sing opera. It's a delightful story, and Disney's animators made full use of the comic aspects of a whale singing at the Met.

The second film of this type, *Fun and Fancy Free*, was released in 1947. In it, Jiminy Cricket opens the film singing a song originally recorded for *Pinocchio*, "I'm a Happy-Go-Lucky Fellow," written by Leigh Harline and Ned Washington.

The film is divided into two parts. In the first, Dinah Shore sings the story of *Bongo*, a circus bear that escapes from the circus to explore the woods. During his adventures, he meets a female bear and falls in love. Later, he finds himself having to battle a massive bear, Lumpjaw, to win his sweetheart. In

Ten unrelated musical short subjects made up Disney's first feature-length film following World War II – *Make Mine Music* – including: (top, left) "The Martins and the Coys;" (top, right) "All the Cats Join In;" (bottom, left) "After You've Gone;" and (bottom, right) "Peter and the Wolf."

Bongo finds out how female bears express their love
in "Say It with a Slap" from the film *Fun and Fancy Free.*

one segment of the short, the female bear slaps
Bongo, which turns out to be the way bears express
their love. Dinah Shore explains in a song written
by Eliot Daniel and Buddy Kaye called "Say It With
A Slap":

*When a bird loves a bird he can twitter,*
*When a puppy falls in love he can yap;*
*Ev'ry pigeon likes to coo when he says, "I love*
*you,"*
*But a bear likes to say it with a slap.*

*When a whippoorwill's in love he can whip-*
*per All the horses neck and all the turtles*
*snap, Ev'ry deer and ev'ry dove has a way of*
*making love*
*But a bear likes to say it with a slap.*

*You can ask any bear,*
*Oh, nothing to compare*
*With a love tap, strong or weak*
*So if you're ready for romance and you ever*
*get the chance,*
*Grab your girl; give her your cheek.*
*So when loves comes along don't be silly,*
*Never waste your time like a sap*
*Let the others hug and kiss but the bare facts*
*are this*
*That a bear likes to say it with a slap, slap.*

In the second part of the film, Disney used the
popular comedian/ventriloquist Edgar Bergen and
his two characters, Charlie McCarthy and Mortimer
Snerd, to provide the narration of a Disney adaptation of "Jack and the Beanstalk." Here, Mickey,
Donald, and Goofy play the heroes and battle the
giant, Willie. Paul Smith did a musical version of
"Fee-Fi-Fo-Fum," which adds to the three cartoon
characters' adventure. The Disney Studio later re-
edited this segment, replacing Edgar Bergen with
Ludwig Von Drake, and released it under the title
"Mickey and the Beanstalk" on television and later
on home video cassette.

A third animated feature, *Melody Time* (1948),
had a similar format to that used in *Make Mine
Music*. It again featured famous names from the field
of entertainment, including Roy Rogers, Ethel
Smith, The Andrews Sisters, Fred Waring and his
Pennsylvanians, Dennis Day, Frances Langford, and
Freddy Martin and his Orchestra. Appropriately, the
film opens with titles shown as pieces of sheet music.

In the opening sequence, Frances Langford
sings "Once Upon a Wintertime" by Bobby Worth
and Ray Gilbert, and the animation features skaters
taken from a greeting card that comes to life. The
next sequence changes tempo with a jazz interpretation of "The Flight of the Bumble Bee" with Freddy
Martin and his Orchestra. Here the animation has
a musical theme, with the bumblebee caught in a
surreal world of musical instruments and symbols.

Jerry Colonna provided the voice of the mighty slugger
Casey in the *Make Mine Music* segment "Casey at the Bat."

Nelson Eddy was the featured performer who provided all of the
voices in the musical comedy "The Whale Who Wanted to Sing at the Met."

Then, Dennis Day tells the story of "Johnny Apple-seed." Two songs in this sequence are noteworthy, "The Lord is Good To Me" and "The Apple Song," both written by Kim Gannon and Walter Kent.

The Andrews Sisters then tell the story through song of "Little Toot," a young tugboat that becomes a hero for saving a ship lost in the storm. In another sequence, Joyce Kilmer's poem "Trees" is set to music and performed by Fred Waring and his Pennsylvanians, a sequence reminiscent of the *Silly Symphony classic*, "The Old Mill."

Joe Carioca and Donald Duck are back together again in "Blame It on the Samba," performed by Ethel Smith on the organ. In one segment, the film combines animation with live action showing Donald and Joe dancing around the organ as Ethel Smith plays. In the final sequence, Roy Rogers tells the story of "Pecos Bill" to Bobby Driscoll and Luana Patten, two child actors who appeared together in *Song of the South* and would be featured in later Disney films.

"Melody Time" was also later re-edited and rereleased as two separate films "Trees and Bumble Boogie" were released as "Contrasts in Rhythm," and the other five sequences were released as *Music Land.*

The final film of this genre is "The Adventures of Ichabod and Mr. Toad," which featured the voices of Bing Crosby and Basil Rathbone. In the first part of the film, Basil Rathbone narrates Kenneth Grahame's "The Wind in the Willows," which is the story of J. Thaddeus Toad's adventures. Some Disney historians consider this sequence to contain some of the finest animation that the studio ever turned out.

The second part of the film consists of Washington Irving's classic tale, "The Legend of Sleepy Hollow," which is narrated by Bing Crosby. In the classic story, the young schoolmaster Ichabod Crane is terrorized by the Headless Horseman. *Time* commented: "The midnight chase through a clutching, echoing forest, with the gangling, lily-livered schoolmaster in full flight before the Headless Horseman, is a skillful blend of the hilarious and the horrible. It is Disney at his facile best."

J. Thaddeus Toad's adventures are related in *The Adventures of Ichabod and Mr. Toad.*

The Headless Horseman from "The Legend of Sleepy Hollow."

With the use of so many well-known entertainers in the Disney films, some observers felt that Walt might be placing too much emphasis on the "star" content of his films. As one of Disney's close associates commented: "For a while, it seemed that Walt forgot that people went to see his films because they were Walt Disney films, not because of who starred in them."

# Live Action and Animation

It was during this period of time that Disney began moving more and more towards live-action films. With the exception of two earlier productions, *The Reluctant Dragon* (1941) and *Victory through Air Power* (1943), the studio had little experience with live action. Although live-action films were less expensive to produce than animated films, there was less control over the action than is possible with animation. However, Walt realized that live-action films could provide the capital necessary to finance the ever-increasing costs of animation, and by the mid-1950s, the studio was producing more live-action films than animated films. The earlier films, which combined live action and animation, enabled the studio to further refine its growing repertoire of film techniques. And, as with his animated films, Walt wanted the absolute best out of live action.

The major film of this era was *Song of the South*, which premiered in Atlanta, Georgia in 1946. Based on native Georgian Joel Chandler Harris' tales of Uncle Remus, the film represented a major advance in animation techniques. With the film, Disney animators were able to further refine the animation technique that placed a living person within the animation sequence. The living person, in this case Uncle Remus, becomes an integral part of the animated scene.

The film essentially tells the story of little Johnny, played by Bobby Driscoll, who is trying to understand his parents' separation. However, the life of the film is found in the sequences with Uncle Remus, played by James Baskett of the popular "Amos 'n' Andy" radio show. He tells Johnny stories about Brer Rabbit's encounters with Brer Fox and Brer Bear. These animated stories are what make this film one of Disney's most enjoyable, as the viewer sees how Brer Rabbit uses cunning and the slow-witted Brer Bear to outwit Brer Fox.

Brer Fox, Brer Rabbit, and Brer Bear from Disney's major postwar film, *Song of the South.*

The entire tone for the film is set in an early sequence where Uncle Remus is beginning to tell Johnny a story. Uncle Remus is shown walking down a country lane, and as he begins to sing "Zip-A-Dee-Doo-Dah," the world is suddenly transformed into an animated world of brilliant color, with fluttering birds and small animals joining him in song. "Zip-A-Dee-Doo-Dah," which was written by Allie Wrubel and Ray Gilbert, and won an Oscar that year, helps set the mood for the film:

Zip-a-dee-doo-dah,
Zip-a-dee-ay,
My, oh my, what a wonderful day!
Plenty of sunshine heading my way,
Zip-a-dee-doo-dah,
Zip-a-dee-ay!
Mister Bluebird's on my shoulder,
It's the truth, it's "actch'll"
Everything is "satisfatch'll"
Zip-a-dee-doo-dah,
Zip-a-dee-ay!
Wonderful feeling,
Wonderful day.

The musical score for *Song of the South* was split between Paul Smith, who did the animated sequences, and Daniele Amfitheatrof, a Russian composer who did the live action. According to Charles Wolcott, who was the film's musical director: "Walt wanted this picture to be superior in every way. He was confident that we could handle the animated segments of the film, but he wanted an experienced composer for the live-action portions. Of course, the irony was that here was Danny, a Russian, scoring a picture about the Deep South, an American phenomenon."

In addition to the song's winning an Oscar, the musical score for the film was nominated with Amfitheatrof, Smith, and Wolcott receiving credit. James Baskett received a special award from the Academy for his portrayal of Uncle Remus. His award reads: "for his able and heartwarming characterization of 'Uncle Remus,' friend and storyteller to the children of the world."

The second live-action/animation film of this era, *So Dear to My Heart* (1949), captured the nostalgic memories of the turn of the century complete with a county fair, Ol' Dan Patch, and the trials and tribulations of a young boy and his pet lamb. It was a lovely and sentimental film that had a special meaning to Walt. He said in an interview, "*So Dear* was especially close to me. Why, that's the life my brother and I grew up with as kids out in Missouri."

A limited amount of animation was used in the film, mainly to highlight the mischievous nature of Jeremiah's pet lamb, Danny. Jeremiah was played by Bobby Driscoll and the film also featured balladeer Burl Ives. The music for the film fit the turn of the century and Burl Ives was ideally chosen to sing the down-home folk songs, among them "Billy Boy" and "Sourwood Mountain." The hit song from the film "Lavender Blue (Dilly Dilly)," written by Larry Morey and Eliot Daniels, was nominated for an Academy Award. Bobby Driscoll was also to receive a special Academy Award for outstanding juvenile.

Walt with Bobby Driscoll on location for the filming of *Song of the South*.

*So Dear To My Heart* featured short animation
sequences, such as this segment with Danny the lamb.

# CHAPTER EIGHT

## Rebirth of Disney Animation

The long-awaited release of *Cinderella* in 1950 marked Disney's return to feature-length animation, and a return to animating the world's favorite fairy tales. During the next ten years, Disney would produce five major animated features, films that more than thirty years later are still considered the standard to which other animated films are compared.

## Cinderella

*Cinderella* was Disney's first animated feature since *Bambi* (1942), and it was an unqualified box-office success, substantially bolstering the studio's sagging financial position. It also marked some musical "firsts." It was the first time that Disney went outside of his own musical staff to hire pop songwriters to compose the songs for an entire picture. The songs from the film were also the first songs to be administered by Disney's own music publishing company. Prior to this, Disney songs were licensed to other music publishers, with Disney

receiving a royalty for their use. Now, with his own publishing company, Disney had greater control over how the songs were promoted. Later, Disney formed his own record companies to further control this important aspect of song promotion.

The songs for *Cinderella* were skillfully developed and effortlessly woven throughout the story. As Leonard Maltin notes in *The Disney Films*: "Songs can literally make or break a film like this, and, in this case, as with most other Disney animated features, the songs enhance the qualities already present and help to establish others that might not be otherwise clear."

In his search for composers, Disney reached into New York's Tin Pan Alley and picked the pop songwriting team of Mack David, Jerry Livingston, and Al Hoffman. Walt first met them in 1947 on a trip to New York. While there, he repeatedly heard a catchy novelty song written by the three entitled "Chi-Baba Chi-Baba" which Perry Como's recording was making famous. Walt invited them to audition for him. As Jerry Livingston recalled: "We played a medley of our songs for Walt, but you could see that he was more interested in 'Chi-Baba.' I think then he had in mind something similar for the fairy godmother's magic scene in *Cinderella*. But he didn't want something ordinary like 'Ali-Kazam.'"

Three months later, the three songwriters were on their way to Hollywood where they would spend the next nine months working on songs for *Cinderella*. As Livingston explained, working on a Disney animated feature was a totally new experience and quite different from other songwriting projects such as films or musicals. First of all, there was no screenplay or script, but instead, there were storyboards that graphically depicted sequences in the film, complete with suggested dialogue. Also, the story was in constant flux. Scenes and sequences were changed daily, with some being dropped even after being fully animated, scored, and filmed. There was a great deal of flexibility with the story, and the animation was regularly modified to accommodate a new song or story idea.

*Opposite:* The songwriting trio for *Cinderella* was comprised of (left to right) Al Hoffman, Mack David and Jerry Livingston.

The first song that the trio of David, Livingston, and Hoffman wrote for *Cinderella* was the beautiful ballad "A Dream Is a Wish Your Heart Makes." As Livingston recalled: "When we went to play it for Walt, he simply said 'That'll work,' and asked us to have a demo record made. We weren't sure of who to use for the vocal, since we were new to Hollywood. Finally, Mack David remembered that Ilene Woods, a singer we knew from the Hit Parade, was now living in Hollywood, so we used her. When Walt heard her voice, he got excited and asked us a lot of questions. The next thing we knew, Ilene was hired for the voice of Cinderella."

The song "A Dream Is A Wish Your Heart Makes" conveys the same message of hope as "When You Wish Upon A Star," and reflects the upbeat nature of Disney music:

*A dream is a wish your heart makes*
*When you're fast asleep.*
*In dreams you will lose your heartaches;*
*Whatever you wish for, you keep.*
*Have faith in your dreams and some day*
*Your rainbow will come smiling thru,*
*No matter how your heart is grieving,*
*if you keep on believing,*
*the dream that you wish will come true.*

Each song in *Cinderella* meticulously fits the action and the story. For "So This Is Love," Paul Smith arranged the song as a duet, and it flows with the action of the Prince and Cinderella at the ball. The novelty number, "Bibbidi-Bobbidi-Boo," helps establish the fairy godmother's slightly bumbling character while still conveying the excitement and fun of transforming Cinderella into a beautifully gowned princess. As Livingston noted, this was the song Walt was looking for when he brought them into the studio. It was nominated for an Academy Award and enjoyed success as a popular hit record.

An interesting technique was used in writing the song "Oh Sing Sweet Nightingale." The writers carried its plaintive tone through, with each successive line of the lyrics containing one less word until the final line of the song, which is simply "Oh."

One particularly difficult assignment was writing "The Work Song." As Livingston recalled: "Walt had in mind some type of ballet sound for the

"The Work Song."

music. But after looking at the storyboards and discussing the action of the animals scurrying about, we knew we needed something light, yet frantic. We did keep Walt's suggestion in mind, and the final song does have a ballet feel to it in the up and down progression of the notes."

"The Work Song" is an example of how a song can contribute to establishing a character and a mood in the film. The bright, fast-paced melody quickly conveys the frenzied atmosphere in which Cinderella works, and the lyrics describe the frustration that she faces.

In the sequence in which Cinderella sadly realizes she has no time to make a dress for the ball, the music and songs are an integral part of telling the story. As her animal friends scurry about to help her, the birds are singing "Cinderella." As the birds and mice go to work gathering scraps of fabric from the sisters' rooms, they sing the tune of "A Dream Is a Wish Your Heart Makes." Leonard Maltin in *The Disney Films* comments: "The sequence of the birds and mice making Cinderella's dress would not work without the key musical numbers that give it direction and tempo. The high-pitched voices of the various animals bring to the rendition an endearing quality that makes it especially memorable."

Cinderella was also a landmark for the Disney organization, since Walt now had his own music publishing company to promote the songs in the film. The RCA album of the film's songs sold more than 750,000 copies in the first year and was a number one seller on *Billboard* magazine's pop album chart, something few children's albums have ever achieved. Single records that were recorded of the songs were equally successful. Perry Como sold over a million copies of his single which featured "A Dream Is a Wish Your Heart Makes" and "Bibbidi-Bobbidi-Boo." The Andrews Sisters had similar success with their recording of "The Work Song." At one point, all three songs were on the Hit Parade, with "Bibbidi" and "A Dream" sharing the two top spots.

In reviewing the film, John Mason Brown noted in the *Saturday Review*: "As 'Bibbidi-Bobbidi-Boo' was being sung, I must admit I rejoiced in something of that same sense of release which all of us used to experience when we responded to 'Who's Afraid of the Big Bad Wolf?,' 'Whistle While You Work,'

'Heigh-Ho,' 'Hi-Diddle-Dee-Dee,' or 'When I See an Elephant Fly.'" *Newsweek* devoted a cover story to the film and called it "the biggest and best news in the American movie industry."

In addition to the Oscar nomination for "Bibbidi-Bobbidi-Boo," the film's musical score, written by Paul Smith and Oliver Wallace, was also nominated.

# Alice in Wonderland

The next year, 1951, *Alice in Wonderland* was released. Disney's fascination with the Lewis Carroll character dates back to the early 1920's when he was producing his *Alice Comedies* featuring black-and-white live action with limited animation. Then, in 1933, the studio considered starring Mary Pickford in a full-length film using live action and animation. In 1945, it was announced that Ginger Rogers would star in the feature film, and finally, in 1946, Walt went ahead with the production of *Alice* as a full-length animated feature.

According to Ward Kimball, an animation director on the film, "I think perhaps the decision to make *Alice* was based 50 percent on the fact that we sorely needed another feature at the time, because a lot of animators had to be kept busy. Disney had many, many artists on the payroll during this period, and he preferred to keep them working on his own projects rather than to let them seek employment elsewhere between features. Surely an economic factor here was the combination of *Alice*'s good name as a famous property and the fact that many animators were out of work. Also, because of the story's episodical nature, Walt could quickly assign different people to different sequences or characters without worrying too much about hook-ups between the sequences."

Since the Carroll tales were separate stories, Disney and his staff enjoyed creative freedom in developing the storyline. In an interview Walt said, "It was imperative that we create a plot structure, for Carroll had not had need for such a thing. We decided, of course, that Alice's curiosity was the only possible prime mover for our story and generator of the necessary suspense. The result is a basic chase pattern that culminates when Alice, after her strange adventures, returns to the world of reality.''

Despite the assignment of directors and animators to different sequences, the film required five years to produce. In the typical Disney demand for authenticity in animation, a live-action film of various segments of *Alice* was first made, using as actors those people whose voices would be used in the animated feature. This gave the animators the opportunity to fully develop the story and create the character nuances that set Disney animated films apart from others.

Seeing how the songs for *Cinderella* were developing, Disney went back to Tin Pan Alley and brought into the studio the songwriting team of Sammy Fain and lyricist Bob Hilliard.

The importance of a song being used to establish the mood and the pace of a film cannot be overstated. A classic example of this is ''I'm Late,'' which occurs early in the film when Alice first meets the White Rabbit. With the song, Fain and Hilliard effectively established the character of the harried rabbit, set the stage for the ensuing madcap scenes that occur later, and provided that ''basic chase pattern'' that Walt wanted. The music is fast-paced and a little frantic, with that feeling carried through in the lyrics:

*I'm late, I'm late for a very important date.*
*No time to say hello, goodbye,*
*I'm late, I'm late, I'm late,*
*No, no, no, no, no, no, I'm overdue,*
*I'm really in a stew,*
*No time to say goodbye, hello,*
*I'm late, I'm late, I'm late.*

In writing this song, Sammy Fain recalled: ''The original version was somewhat different, not as hurried. We had played it for Walt and he liked it. But that night I kept thinking about it and finally wrote out a second version. The next day I got in to

The White Rabbit is frantic in the song "I'm Late" from *Alice in Wonderland.*

Walt with Kathryn Beaumont, the voice of Alice.

The songwriting team of Sammy Fain (top) and Bob Hilliard (bottom) composed the music for *Alice in Wonderland.*

see Walt and played it for him, and he was delighted. There are few studios I know of where you could get in to see the top man and have him change his mind on a song."

Fain's instrumental "March of the Cards" came about almost by accident. As he recalled: "I had this two-bar intro, or 'vamp,' that I was using for another song, and Walt heard it one day. He came over and said, 'Sammy, I like that. I think it would fit with the cards marching. Do you think you can do something with it?' So I took this vamp, really a throwaway line, and worked it into the march. Walt impressed me with his uncanny ear for what type of music would work in his pictures."

One of the toughest sequences of *Alice* was the Mad Tea Party. No one was able to come up with a theme, a song, or even a reason for it. As was Walt's style, he involved everyone at the studio in solving such problems. The *Cinderella* songwriting team of David, Livingston, and Hoffman were still at the studio and they became involved. As Jerry Livingston remembers: "One day Walt asked us to give it some thought even though we weren't on the picture. Here was a ten-to fifteen-minute major scene that they still didn't know how to handle. Finally, Mack David came up with the 'un-birthday' idea. Since there are 364 un-birthday days each year, it was a perfect reason for a mad tea party. And, it fit perfectly with the more-than-mad hatter."

There were other problems associated with the Mad Tea Party scene. Ward Kimball recalled: "After the script had been written, and we had what we thought was a good pre-recorded dialogue track, we decided to shoot a rough black-and-white live-action version to serve only as an inspiration for my animation, and from which I could select any bits and business that I might choose to re-work into animation. For this live-action test we decided to use Ed Wynn, who had provided the voice of the Mad Hatter. The problem was, Ed had trouble following the playback that had been recorded by himself. It drove him crazy. Sitting there with his big hat among all those knives, forks, and tea-cups, he said, 'I can't do it. Why don't you turn that darn voice-track thing off, and I'll remember roughly what I said.' We agreed by saying, 'OK, we'll just use one little mike with no attempt at fidelity to pick-up what you say so Ward can later identify the action.'

Walt reviews the musical score for Alice with its composer, Oliver Wallace.

"Well, the nonsense stuff that Ed ad-libbed on that sound stage was a lot funnier than some of the recorded stuff that we had carefully written out for him. When Walt saw the black-and-white test he said, 'Let's use that soundtrack! That's great!' The sound department hit the fan, complaining '... we can't use that test-track; there's too much background noise! To which Walt simply replied, 'That's your problem!' and walked out of the room."

Nonsense songs and novelty songs abounded in *Alice*, including Fain and Hilliard's "The Caucus Race" and "Old Father William." Oliver Wallace composed "A E I O U" and Don Raye wrote "Twas Brillig" with Gene DePaul.

The musical score for *Alice*, written by Oliver Wallace, was nominated for an Academy Award. Hollis Alpert, in the *Saturday Review*, called it "catchy and likable." *Newsweek* wrote: "One of the most successful sequences involves the song 'All in the Golden Afternoon' and an imaginative, Silly Symphony-like garden of live flowers." And Philip Hartung, in *Commonweal*, called the film "bright and fresh and imaginative."

# Peter Pan

When *Peter Pan* was released in 1953, it fulfilled a long-time dream of Walt's, since *Peter Pan* had always occupied a special place in his heart. As he explained it: "When I began producing cartoons, *Peter Pan* was high on my list of subjects. In fact, after talking it over, Roy and I bought the rights with the idea of making it the second full-length feature for our company. Actually, it was a long time before we began work on the story. In the first place, I was unwilling to start until I could do full justice to the well-loved story. Animation techniques were constantly improving, but they still fell short of what I felt was needed to tell the story of Peter Pan as I saw it.

"Next to *Snow White*, I cared most for Peter Pan. He did not come from our well-loved storybooks, but my introduction to him was even more exciting. We were living on a farm, and one morning as we walked to school, we found entrancing new posters on the barns and fences along the road. A road company was coming to the nearby town of Marceline, and the play they were presenting was *Peter Pan* with Maude Adams.

"It took most of the contents of two toy savings banks to buy tickets, but my brother Roy and I didn't care. For two hours we lived in Never Land with Peter and his friends. I took many memories away from the theater with me, but the most thrilling of all was the vision of Peter flying through the air."

Walt acquired the rights for the James Barrie play in 1939. The film did not go into production until 1949, taking four years to produce at a cost of more than $3 million—the most expensive film to date that Disney had produced.

Sticking with the Tin Pan Alley songwriters that he had used previously, Disney brought back Sammy Fain along with Sammy Cahn to do most of the songs for the film. Oliver Wallace handled the musical score, with Ed Plumb doing the orchestrations. The choral arrangements in the film were directed by Jud Conlon.

Although the songs from *Peter Pan* were not major hits, they were skillfully used within the story. Early in the film, Peter Pan explains that Never Land

is located near "The Second Star to the Right," a song reminiscent of the other Disney songs of dreams and hopes. When the children ask Peter Pan how to get to Never Land, he instructs them how to fly by speaking the words of the song "You Can Fly, You Can Fly, You Can Fly." The children respond by speaking, while the orchestra plays phrases from the tune complete with various instrumental effects such as harp glissandi, string tremolos, and high flutes to suggest the magical and buoyant mood of the scene. Then, as they begin to follow Peter over the rooftops of London, the chorus sings.

Leonard Maltin, commenting on the film in *The Disney Films*, writes: "Students of the musical film would do well to study *Peter Pan*, not only to hear the beautiful choral arrangements by Jud Conlon, but to observe how masterfully the musical element of the film was integrated into the story. When the children ask Peter how they get to Never Land, he tells them it's easy, and begins to speak the lyrics of 'You Can Fly.' The kids join him, speaking

Kathryn Beaumont with Disney artist John Hench.

rhythmically, but naturally, and almost, but never quite, bursting into song; the actual singing is taken up by the chorus, as the children fly out of the nursery window and into the night. Throughout the rest of the film, songs are introduced, and sometimes sung, in fragments, or so naturally that one is hardly aware they have begun. Even in the midst of Wendy's tender song 'Your Mother and Mine,' action is continuing, as Captain Hook's crew gathers outside the hide-out to capture the Lost Boys."

The one song that did gain some popularity from the film was "Never Smile at a Crocodile" by Frank Churchill with lyrics by Jack Lawrence. However, the lyrics are never sung in the film, but rather, the melody is used to announce the presence of the crocodile. The animated character of Tinker Bell in the film went on to become a television star, as Disney used her as the opening for his weekly television series.

Jon Newsom used the "You Can Fly" sequence of the film in his "A Sound Idea: Music for Animated Films" to discuss the complexities involved in producing animated films. He writes: "What the viewer sees and hears is the roughly three minutes of the finished sequence, which required the coordinated decisions and skills of many people, including the writers and the actors who recorded the script; the sound effects department; the composers and arrangers who provided just the right amount as well as the right kind of music required to accompany the action; the singers and orchestra musicians who recorded the music; the animators who, with fully developed character models before them, drew them in action to synchronize with pre-recorded voices, songs, instrumental music, sound effects, and pre-established actions; the inkers and color artists who traced and colored the animator's drawings on the transparent cels that are used in the final frame-by-frame photography; the background artists who painted whatever stationary scenery was required for the animated figures; and the cameraman who made the finished film with the guidance of an exposure sheet containing instructions for shooting the backgrounds, cels, and visual effects which are achieved by moving the camera closer to or farther away from the artwork for each exposure. A mistake on one exposure would throw the entire film out of synchronization with the soundtrack, or would result in other breakdowns in the coherence of the picture which would be costly to repair."

Tinker Bell went on to become a television star by opening Disney's weekly series.

"Never Smile at a Crocodile."

# Lady and the Tramp

For the next animated feature, *Lady and the Tramp* (1955), Disney departed from his proven formula of using classical children's stories. He selected a story with the same title by Ward Greene. The film provided a preview of the direction that Walt would take with his animated films. With the exception of *Sleeping Beauty*, which was in the beginning stages of production at this time, Walt would no longer draw upon the fairy tales from his childhood as the source for his films. Also, *Lady* was done with a different style of animation, a style that more closely approximated real life, and used colors that were more muted than in earlier films. This same style would be used in later years on *The Fox and the Hound* and *The Rescuers*.

Walt had selected songstress Peggy Lee to be the voice for the supporting characters, and Barbara Luddy for the voice of Lady. As she became more and more involved with her part and attended the various storyboard meetings, Peggy Lee's enthusiasm and excitement about the film led to her suggestions of song possibilities within the story. As a result, Walt teamed her with songwriter Sonny Burke to write all of the songs for the picture. In addition, Miss Lee did many of the vocals for the songs, including the duet for "Siamese Cat Song." The versatility of her voice carried her from the ballad-like "La-La-Lu" to the Oriental-sounding cat song to a torchy jazz sound in the song "He's a Tramp."

The film is delightful from many aspects. It has an appealing storyline about how a dog (Tramp) from the wrong side of the tracks wins the hearts and affections of Lady's animal friends and her owners through his heroic actions. There are enchanting sequences within the film, particularly one in which Lady has been taken to the pound, and is told through song that Tramp is a ladies' man. The entire action of the dogs within the pound is comical and endearing.

Peggy Lee and Sonny Burke wrote all of the songs
for *Lady and the Tramp*, and Miss Lee did many
of the vocals for the songs.

Leonard Maltin, in *The Disney Films*, commented: "Most of the film's best sequences are built around songs, and the film's score is particularly delightful, as written by Peggy Lee and Sonny Burke, and in several cases, sung by Miss Lee, who does the voices for Darling, the Siamese Cats, and Peg."

The music in *Lady* gracefully highlights the action. Oliver Wallace's score for the film opens with a full choral rendition of "Bella Notte" backed with a full orchestra. As the titles dissolve, a wintry Christmas scene is set with a moving tenor solo "Peace on Earth."

When a baby enters Lady's household, the ballad "La-La-Lu (What's a Baby)" is used effectively not only to establish Lady's confusion, but also to carry the action of the film. Next, Aunt Sarah arrives with her cunning and mischievous Siamese cats. The lyrics of the song "We are Siamese if you please, we are Siamese if you don't please," help establish the cats' characters and show that Lady's peaceful home is changing.

After Lady runs away from home and encounters Tramp, one of the most charming scenes in the film takes place. The two dogs are shown sharing a romantic spaghetti dinner, serenaded by the restaurant's owner, Tony, singing "Bella Notte" accompanied by mandolins. As the dogs stroll in the moonlight to a choral version of the song in the background, Tramp does a Bogart imitation with his line: "There's a big world out there and it's ours for the taking."

A favorite scene of Walt's was the one in which the dogs in the pound howl to the melody of "Home Sweet Home." He had a tape of it which he frequently played for guests at this home. No words are used, just the vocal group yapping and howling to the melody.

*Lady*, rereleased for the 1986 Christmas season, is another Disney film that has not been generally released for television. It joins a select group of films that include *Snow White*, *Fantasia*, *Bambi*, *Song of the South*, *Peter Pan*, and *Cinderella*, to name several.

"The Siamese Cat Song."

"Bella Notte."

# Sleeping Beauty

Walt's final animated film of the decade was *Sleeping Beauty* (1959). This was a film that he had started in 1950 and had to sideline for a few years because of time commitments for Disneyland and his three television series. When the film was finally completed, it had cost Disney more than $6 million, making it the most expensive animated cartoon up to that time.

Visually, the film lives up to its $6 million price tag. Although not a box office triumph in its initial release, it has become very popular in rerelease and in the home video market.

The release of *Sleeping Beauty* also marked the end of an era for Disney and the studio—it was the last time that Disney would use a classic children's story as the basis for an animated feature. Audience tastes were changing and it was difficult for Disney's creative staff to work within the tight confines imposed by well-known stories, being restricted by how liberally they could interpret a story. Still another factor was that Disney had already done the more popular fairy tales.

For the music, George Bruns, who had joined the studio a few years earlier, was given the assignment of taking Tchaikovsky's *Sleeping Beauty* ballet and adapting it for the film. Bruns was a versatile writer and had been previously involved with the "Mr. Magoo" cartoon series.

Jon Newsom, in his "A Sound Idea: Music in Animated Films," commented: "The dramatic music for Disney's animated features remained at a high level—even when the music was not by a Disney composer. In his last animated feature, *Sleeping Beauty*, conceived in 1950 and released in 1959,

Walt with the storyboards for *Sleeping Beauty*.

as Disney's ultimate and most expensive achievement in animation, George Bruns arranged Tchaikovsky's ballet score based on the story by Charles Perrault. For anyone who has never composed music, and for whom the whole process of composing seems utterly mystifying, the recourse to using, by skillful rearrangement, pre-existing music may seem an easy way out. That is not necessarily true. Indeed, unlike arranging the kind of music made for travelogues that has the consistency and spreadability of whipped margarine, the bending, the cutting and welding of such cohesive stuff as a major work of Tchaikovsky's can be more difficult than starting from scratch."

In an interview with George Bruns, he explained that about one-third of the musical score for *Sleeping Beauty* was Bruns emulating Tchaikovsky. He explained, "There were a number of liberties that I had to take with Tchaikovsky's original work, since the music did not fit what was taking place on the screen. Unless someone were a student of Tchaikovsky, you cannot tell the difference in the film."

One of the first sequences that Bruns scored was a portion of the Bluebird scene during which Princess Aurora, in the guise of Briar Rose, is gathering berries in the forest with her animal friends. As one studio observer recalled: "When *Sleeping Beauty* went into work, George Bruns was brought in to score the picture. He wrote some music for a sequence. Walt was called in to view it. Walt had never met Bruns. They ran the sequence and Walt said: 'Looks good . . . and the music sounds great.' Someone suddenly realized that Walt hadn't met Bruns, so he said, 'Oh, by the way Walt—this is George Bruns who is doing the music for *Sleeping Beauty*.' George stood up to acknowledge the introduction— all 6'3'' and 250 pounds of him. Walt looked at him in surprise and said: 'I'm glad I didn't say anything bad about the music.'"

By this time, Disney had become the master at merchandising his films. To promote *Sleeping Beauty*, he licensed 55 companies to manufacture more than 100 "Sleeping Beauty" items, including a Princess Aurora doll, a Prince's hat complete with plume-shaped pen, games, puppets, jewelry, and even babies' diapers. There were 2.1 million *Sleeping Beauty* comic books and more than 5 million hardbound books. Fourteen different *Sleeping Beauty* records were produced.

Bruns' score for the picture was nominated for an Academy Award. In its review of the film, *Newsweek* commented, "Disney does it again."

Princess Aurora sings "I Wonder."

# CHAPTER NINE

## *New Worlds of Entertainment*

The decade of the Fifties saw Disney go beyond animated cartoons to new worlds of entertainment. During this time, Walt dramatically increased production of live-action films, successfully ventured into that relatively new entertainment medium called "television," and gambled every dime he had on developing and building an amusement park that met his exacting standards— Disneyland. Without a doubt, this era amply demonstrated that Walt Disney was an entertainment genius, and in every direction that he took, music was to play a vital role.

# Treasure Island

Disney's first totally live-action film, *Treasure Island*, was released in 1950. The use of Robert Louis Stevenson's popular adventure story was in keeping with Disney's practice of using material that was known to his audiences. *Treasure Island* was filmed in England, primarily out of economic necessity, since Disney had funds "frozen" there that could not be taken out of the country. As a result, three other films were produced in England — *The Story of Robin Hood* (1952), *The Sword and the Rose* (1953), and *Rob Roy* (1954).

Disney did not scrimp on the music for any of these films. John Huntley, in his article "The Music of Treasure Island" in *Film Music*, writes: "Under the general supervision of Muir Mathieson (music director to the production), Mrs. Buck, his personal assistant, conducted a research during which over three hundred sea shanties and old maritime songs were examined before a final selection was submit-

ted to the production chief, Perce Pearce. It was essential that the songs chosen should not only be correct for the period (1765), but also that they should be suitable in lilt and tempo to the scenes involved. Walt Disney himself heard a number of test recordings before the final selection was made."

Even after all this effort, only fragments of the shanties are used in the film. Clifton Parker, who wrote the score for *Treasure Island* and the other English productions, commented: "*Treasure Island* has proved to be a most interesting task. First of all, there was the little matter of sea shanties. You have heard how one or two are sung in the film. Then came the great point—should they come into the main musical score . . . it was found impossible to use them because they were too recognizably tuneful. They broke through the action and would have claimed too much of the audience's attention." To further enhance the musical quality of the film, Disney used the prestigious Royal Philharmonic Orchestra for the soundtrack.

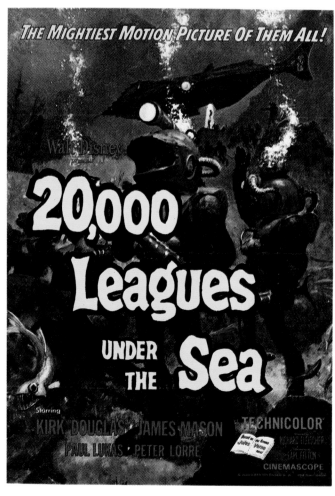

In 1954, Disney decided to enter the field of television and began producing a weekly one-hour show. Though it did go through many name changes and all three networks, the show became the longest-running prime-time show on television. The television show was given the same attention and effort that went into Disney films. Disney's insistence on quality had several side benefits, one of which was that several of the shows developed for television were later released as full-length theatrical feature films. The television show also gave Disney a vehicle in which to promote his films and, very important to Disney, to promote and finance his new venture—Disneyland.

# 20,000 Leagues under the Sea

Disney's first domestic live-action film, released in 1954, was based on Jules Verne's novel *20,000 Leagues under the Sea*. In typical Disney fashion, the studio developed special effects for the film that were years ahead of the industry, and Disney's special effects department was presented with an Academy Award for their efforts.

Prior to the release of the film, Disney aired *Operation Undersea*, a documentary about the filming of *20,000 Leagues*, on his weekly television show. Although some critics labeled it a crass one-hour commercial for the film, it won an Emmy for the best television show of the season.

*20,000 Leagues* starred James Mason, Kirk Douglas, Paul Lucas, and Peter Lorre. In the film, Kirk Douglas did his own vocal on a bright sea shanty written by Al Hoffman and Norman Gimbel, "A Whale of a Tale." The musical score for the film was handled by Paul Smith, who developed an eerie underwater effect that stands out today as a unique means of achieving this mood. He explained, "I used a combination of low strings and woodwinds, piano, harp, gong, and I found an orchestra bass marimba that could reach the lowest F on the piano. Together, they provide the perfect underwater effect."

# Davy Crockett

The synergism between Disney's television show and his films was never more evident than during the "Davy Crockett" boom. The success of Davy Crockett caught the studio totally by surprise, and even Walt admitted: "We had no idea what was going to happen to 'Crockett.' Why, by the time the first show finally got on the air, we were already filming the third one and calmly killing Davy off at the Alamo. It became one of the biggest overnight hits in TV history, and there we were with just three films and a dead hero."

The man responsible for the show's theme song, "The Ballad of Davy Crockett," was George Bruns. Bruns had joined the studio in 1953 and spent more than twenty years on the studio's music staff. Although his background had been primarily in jazz, he proved to be an extremely versatile composer, moving easily from the symphonic sounds of *Sleeping Beauty* to the lively operetta adaptation of Victor Herbert's *Babes in Toyland*, the first live-action musical picture the studio produced, to rollicking Western songs.

Frank Thomas and Ollie Johnston, in their book *Disney Animation*, write: "The best music was achieved when it could springboard from the hours of thought and refinement that had gone into the story development and acting. If a sequence is well balanced, builds properly, has life, good textures, and a flow, the musician has a much better chance of writing a superior score than if the picture is dull, lifeless, and spotty. Even the grandest score will seem unimpressive under those conditions.

"With a smaller crew and extended schedules for the pictures of the sixties and seventies, it was no longer possible to keep a musician on full time, so we shared one with the live action units. George Bruns worked equally well in either medium, writing 'Davy Crockett' for the live TV show at the same time he was adapting Tchaikovsky's ballet score for *Sleeping Beauty* to our animated version. George was big and easy-going, but he worked very hard and produced a seemingly endless string of fresh melodies and haunting scores.

George Bruns (on the trombone) wrote the music for "The Ballad of Davy Crockett," which became one of the biggest Disney songs ever.

"He did temp tracks, prescored some selections, orchestrated songs, jumped over to the live action shows, then back to consult on the best musical treatment for the next sequence in the cartoon. When there was more to do than he could handle, he suggested we find a piece of music from an earlier movie and 'track' our picture with that. It enabled us to find just the mood we wanted, the tempos and phrasing to support our action, and kept us from wearing him out.

"When the time came to write the final score, George was fresh and enthusiastic, suggesting more effective ways to present our concepts, and writing lovely new ballads in the same tempo and feeling as the ones we used for our 'tracking.'"

*Davy Crockett* had originally been planned as a three-part film on the "Frontierland" episodes of the Disney TV show. During the production of *Davy Crockett*, Walt asked Bruns to come up with a "throwaway" tune that could be used to bridge the time gaps in the story. What Walt needed was a song that would carry the story from one sequence to the other. It took Bruns about thirty minutes to write the melody line and the chorus—"Davy, Davy Crockett, king of the wild frontier." Tom Blackburn, a scriptwriter at the studio who had never written a song lyric previously, supplied the lyrics.

The original song ran a full twenty stanzas of six lines each, with every stanza telling the continuing story of Davy's exploits. The formal song title is actually: "The Ballad of Davy Crockett: His Early Life, Hunting Adventures, Services under General Jackson in the Creek War, Electioneering Speeches, Career in Congress, Triumphal Tour in the Northern States, and Services in the Texan War."

In the book *Davy Crockett: The Man, The Legend, The Legacy, 1786-1986*, edited by Michael A. Lofaro, Charles K. Wolfe writes in "Davy Crockett Songs: Minstrels to Disney": "By the end of February 1955, even before the biggest part of the Crockett

boom hit, singers were racing into the studios to do their versions of the catchy song. Within a few weeks, versions of the song had hit the *Billboard* charts—pop music's best trade barometer—in three categories: pop, country and western, and children's. Apparently the first pop singer to record the song was the man who in the end had the most popular version of it: Bill Hayes. Hayes was an unlikely candidate for the honor; an Illinois native, he had had previous experience in light opera and as a comic actor on the old 'Ernie Kovacs' television show; in more recent years he has become known as a character actor on soap operas. Hayes recorded 'The Ballad of Davy Crockett' for a new independent record label called Cadence—a rather small label that would later win fame as the company to make first recordings of national stars like the Everly Brothers and Andy Williams—and watched with amazement as the disc sold over two million copies in six months' time. For twenty weeks, the Hayes version stayed on the best-seller charts and for five weeks it was the number one hit in the United States, where it contended with the Four Aces' 'Love Is a Many-Splendored Thing' and the Chordettes' 'Mr. Sandman.' Though most of the song's popularity undoubtedly had to do with the Crockett films, part of it also came on the crest of a popular revival of folk music. . . 'The Ballad of Davy Crockett' attracted over twenty such cover versions by singers from every corner of American music: country/western singers Tennessee Ernie Ford, Mac Wiseman, Rusty Draper, The Sons of the Pioneers, Eddy Arnold, and Burl Ives; mainstream pop artists like Steve Allen, Vincent Lopez, Mitch Miller, Walter Schumann, and Fred Waring; and even jazz musicians like the Irwin Fields Trio and Paul Smith. Fess Parker, the star of the Disney films, made a recording of the piece himself for Columbia, one of the country's major labels, and saw it sell close to one million copies in just under a month. . . in six months the combined record sales, from all versions, were close to 7,000,000—making it, according to discographer Joseph Murrells, 'the fastest selling entity in the history of the disc industry.'"

The original two stanzas of the blockbuster song "The Ballad of Davy Crockett" went as follows:

*Born on a mountain top in Tennessee,*
*Greenest state in the Land of the Free.*
*Raised in the woods so's he knew ev'ry tree*
*Kilt him a b'ar when he was only three.*
*Davy, Davy Crockett,*
*King of the wild frontier.*

*In eighteen thirteen the Creeks uprose,*
*addin' redskin arrows to the country's woes.*
*Now Injun fightin' is somethin' he knows*
*so he shoulders his rifle an' off he goes.*
*Davy, Davy Crockett*
*King of the wild frontier.*

"Crockettmania" swept the country by storm, launching an astonishing marketing phenomenon that Disney used to full advantage. Everywhere you went, there were coonskin hats (a presidential candidate, Senator Estes Kefauver from Tennessee, even used it as his campaign symbol), jeans, lunch buckets, and hundreds of Davy Crockett-imprinted items. *Time* magazine estimated that, within months, more than $100 million in Davy Crockett merchandise had been sold. "The Ballad of Davy Crockett" spent more than six months on the Hit Parade, was recorded on more than two hundred record labels around the world, and sold more than ten million records.

Bruns noted that the success of the Davy Crockett phenomenon was a big boost to Disney's finances, especially coming on the heels of the huge expenses involved with building Disneyland and producing the television shows. In commenting on the song, Bruns said: "It certainly took everybody at the studio by surprise. The irony of it was that most people thought it was an authentic folk song that we had uncovered and updated. Usually, when you have a hit song, there are always lawsuits claiming prior authorship. In the case of 'Davy Crockett,' not a single suit was filed."

The success of *Davy Crockett* spawned an explosion of Westerns on television and in the movies throughout the film industry. The three-part television series was edited and a feature film was released in 1955 as *Davy Crockett, King of the Wild Frontier.* Leonard Maltin, in *The Disney Films*, commented: "Finally, it was decided to take advantage of the

Crockett boom and splice the three one-hour programs into a feature film for theatrical release, just in time for summer vacation. Here is where Disney's policy of turning out quality TV programming paid off, for the finished product, trimmed to ninety minutes, hardly betrays its television origin—a neat trick that few other producers could have pulled off. Disney also had the foresight to film his series in color."

Disney produced a sequel, *Davy Crockett and the River Pirates* (1956), which was also comprised of episodes originally filmed for the television show. Fess Parker became a familiar face in Disney productions, starring in such films as *The Great Locomotive Chase* (1956), *Westward Ho the Wagons* (1956), and *Old Yeller* (1957). Other Westerns or historically-oriented films that were produced by Disney during this time included *Johnny Tremain* (1957), *The Light in the Forest* (1958), and *Tonka* (1958).

Still another made-for-television series also made it into the theaters as *The Sign of Zorro* (1960). The title song, which was written by George Bruns and Norman Foster, became a familiar tune around the country, but neither the character nor the song came close to the popularity of *Davy Crockett*.

# The True-Life Adventure Series

During this time, Disney was also having critical success with a series of documentary short subjects that he released under the "True-Life Adventure" nature series. In *The Disney Films*, Leonard Maltin explained: "Disney's greatest, and most surprising, success in the late 1940s and 1950s, however, was with a series of nature films. For years, it was claimed that this came about by chance, when Walt was vacationing in Alaska and happened to meet camera store owners Alfred and Elma Milotte, who impressed him with their amateur wildlife movies. The truth is that Disney hatched the idea himself and then went looking for someone to bring it to life. Emery F. Tobin, publisher of *The Alaska Sportsman* magazine, recommended the Milottes, who were on tour in Los Angeles at the time, showing their wildlife films. Disney contracted for footage on Alaskan seals, and the results were edited down to a half-hour color short called *Seal Island*. Even Disney's brother, Roy, tried to discourage this project, as there was no interest from

*The African Lion,* one of the feature films in the *True-Life Adventure* nature series.

theater owners at all. But Disney got it shown in one Los Angeles area theater to qualify for an Academy Award—and it won! It became a tremendous critical and financial success, and led to a long-running *True-Life Adventure* series that eventually expanded to feature length.''

The roots for the *True-Life Adventure* series can be traced back to *Bambi*. At that time, Walt had live animals brought into the studio so that the animators could study them to better understand how the animals moved. Walt explained, ''. . . in studying the animals, we brought deer in, brought them into the art classes and let 'em munch hay and things to keep them quiet and the artists were drawing the animals. But that wasn't enough. We had to see 'em more as they actually behaved in nature. And I found a naturalist photographer that had done some beautiful work out in the open country, and I made a deal with him to go and cover the action of the animals as they actually lived their lives. And he went into the Maine country. And he went into different parts of the country where he could find animals and photographed them for me. And he caught 'em just living their lives as nature intended. And that was the start. I said, 'We can't invent those things. It's only the animals themselves can think 'em up.' And that started my whole nature series.''

The background score for these films were a key element in their success. Paul Smith was responsible for the music in most of these films. In an interview, he explained: ''In the *True-Life* series, music seeks to complement the pictorial scene by pacing the picture, by pointing up the action, and by making the emotional content more poignant. The music attempts, in a sympathetic way, to give the 'critters' seemingly human characteristics that will be recognized by a theater audience. The balance of the characters—the hero, the villain, the ingenue, etc.,—are described in musical terms.''

Working on the nature films was quite different than scoring animated features. Smith explained he had to work with a fully edited film, in many instances, he did not have the ability, as he did with animation, to change or alter the scenes to fit the music. Rather, he had to write his music to fit the action precisely. However, there were occasions where the film was edited with the music in mind.

such as repeating certain animal movements that would coincide with the beat of the music.

Disney produced thirteen *True-Life Adventure* films, eight of which won Oscars. The Oscar-winning films were: *Seal Island* (1949), *Beaver Valley* (1950), *Nature's Half Acre* (1951), *Water Birds* (1952), *Bear Country* (1953), *The Living Desert* (1953), *The Vanishing Prairie* (1954), and *White Wilderness* (1958). In addition, Paul Smith's score for *Perri* (1957)—a *True-Life Fantasy* film—was nominated for an Academy Award, as was Oliver Wallace's score the next year for *White Wilderness*.

The first film in this series scored by Paul Smith was *Beaver Valley*, and his past experience with synchronizing music and action in animated films was readily apparent. James Algar, the director assigned to *Beaver Valley*, wrote in an article in *Film Music*: ''There is one thing perhaps which sets the *Beaver Valley* score apart from others of its kind. I believe that one of the reasons the music is effective is the fact that we used an animated cartoon technique in a live-action film. Musically speaking, I mean by this that we synchronized our music to our screen pantomine more often and more closely than is generally done in live-action movies. This was attempted not only in the major sequences where the ducks quacked to a tempo and the frogs croaked in unison with the orchestra, but all the way through the picture in little individual situations.

''To get this close synchronization requires patience, time and careful planning. It involves a thorough study of the picture by the composer. It means running the picture back and forth on a Movieola while the action is observed scene by scene; it means timing these actions with a stop-watch; it means coping with the mathematics of the problem of so many feet passing through the projector in so many seconds accompanied by so many bars of music to such and such a tempo.''

Smith was very successful with this technique, for as *Time* noted in its review of the film: ''Paul Smith's score is a miracle of synchronization and human comment. The film's *piece de resistance*: the frogs and crickets croaking and chirping through a chorus of the sextet from *Lucia*.'' *Newsweek* added: ''With the aid of Winston Hibler's tasteful and humorous narration and Paul Smith's eloquent background music, the entire cast, which includes also crickets, tree frogs, and a goggle-eyed great blue heron, become tragic, comical, and often near-human personalities."

The series had its humorous touches which were heightened with music. In *The Vanishing Prairie*, prairie dogs accompany a barbershop quartet rendition of "Home on the Range." A battle of bighorn rams is coupled with "The Anvil Chorus." A jack rabbit's getaway, shown in slow motion, has a jazz beat that precisely matches the leg action used to avoid tight places.

In commenting on *The Vanishing Prairie*, Philip Hamburger wrote in *The New Yorker*, ". . . there are also winter scenes, spring scenes, high clouds, cloudbursts, animals fighting animals, buffaloes sadly moving across the plains, and the long lonesome plains themselves." And, Paul Smith's brilliant score beautifully captured all of these moods.

In *Nature's Half Acre*, Smith used a springtime waltz to set the mood, with the music following the tempo of a cedar waxwing bouncing on a branch. In a scene where caterpillars are chewing leaves, the motion of their jaws establishes the musical tempo. For a praying mantis, Smith uses a "bogeyman" theme. In *The Living Desert*, the courtship of the scorpions resembles a square dance, which is exactly the type of music Smith used to accompany the scene.

An expansion of the *True-Life Adventure* concept was *Perri*, a story tracing the life of a young squirrel, based on *Bambi* author Felix Salten's book of the same title. *Perri* was called a *True-Life Fantasy*, since liberties were taken to fit the film around the story, and animation was used to illustrate a dream sequence.

As *Time* commented: "The musical score of the film is everything a squirrel could ask for. When the animals sleep, a choir of angels breathes over them, which sounds almost like 'Brahms' Lullaby,' but turns out to be an original composition of George Bruns, the man who wrote 'Davy Crockett.' When Perri sleeps, she dreams in a combination of live and animated effects, just like the other movie stars; then the dream figures engage in the usual elaborate ballet—though of course they are not people, but dear little bunnies."

Other nature films included (top to bottom) *Perri*, *Beaver Valley*, and *The Living Desert*. The latter two films won Oscars, and Paul Smith's score for *Perri* was nominated for an Academy Award.

# The Mickey Mouse Club

Disney's second television venture, *The Mickey Mouse Club*, was also a success. Launched in 1955, the show became an instant hit, and every weekday, the familiar "M-I-C-K-E-Y M-O-U-S-E" blasted forth from the nation's television sets as children rushed home from school to see Annette, Cubby, Darlene, and the rest of the Mouseketeers. The key to the show was the talented Jimmie Dodd, who composed many of the songs used on the show, including the title song. Also contributing to the show was Buddy Baker, who had joined the studio following a successful career with the big bands and radio.

As Baker recalled: "This was a hectic time at the studio. We had the weekly series to write music for, plus the daily show. This was in addition to the feature films the studio was producing. And, Walt demanded quality, whether it was music for a multi-million dollar animated feature or our daily television show."

Baker became a mainstay of the studio's music staff and has been involved with composing the music for many of the attractions at Disneyland and Walt Disney World. He also continued to write music for Disney's television shows, and in 1973, his score for the feature film *Napoleon and Samantha* received an Academy Award nomination.

In 1977, the Disney studio launched *The New Mickey Mouse Club* in an attempt to recapture the halcyon days of the Fifties. However, the audience for the show, as well as the expenses, did not justify its continuance. Of note though is a young man who had appeared on an early *Mickey Mouse Club* Talent Roundup, Bob Brunner, who was now a part of the Disney music staff and wrote many of the songs used on the new show.

Jimmie Dodd and Annette Funicello of *The Mickey Mouse Club*.

# Disneyland

The opening of Disneyland in Anaheim, California in 1955 marked the culmination of a dream for Walt Disney. When his daughters were young, Disney despaired at the death of amusement parks that were family-oriented and enjoyable to parents as well as children. In the ensuing years, he visited amusement parks throughout the world looking for ideas on what an ideal park should have.

Disney was so committed to this project that he originally undertook it on his own and not as part of the studio, borrowing heavily to finance it. Walt even struck a deal with the American Broadcasting Company (ABC) for part of the financing, but he later bought ABC's interest back at a substantial profit to the broadcasting company. Many called it "Disney's Folly," as some had dubbed his plans for *Snow White* twenty years earlier.

a new kind of HORROR movie...
HORRIBLY FUNNY!
I WAS A TEEN-AGE BOY!
You'll love "SHAGGY" the shaggiest of all shaggy dogs!
WALT DISNEY'S
the SHAGGY DOG
STARRING
Fred MacMURRAY · Jean HAGEN
TOMMY KIRK · ANNETTE FUNICELLO · TIM CONSIDINE · KEVIN "MOOCHIE" CORCORAN
with
CECIL KELLAWAY · ALEXANDER SCOURBY
ROBERTA SHORE · JAMES WESTERFIELD and JACQUES AUBUCHON

Disneyland opened as a tremendous success and continues to be successful. Since the opening of the California park, the Disney organization has opened Walt Disney World in Florida and a Disneyland in Tokyo, with another theme park planned for Europe.

On Disneyland's tenth anniversary, *Newsweek* commented: "It took a Disney to think of building a real (well, almost) Mississippi River stern-wheeler, to build a scale model of the Matterhorn and a Sleeping Beauty's castle, to put up a gently nostalgic Main-Street-that-never-was and simply let people enjoy it. It took Disney to adapt cartoon animation to the amusement-park field filling Disneyland with charging plastic hippopotamuses, prowling Indians and singing flowers. And it took Disney to find the proper blend: the excitement of a head-snapping bobsled ride down the Matterhorn, the serenity of a gentle boat ride past the Lilliputian villages of Story Book Land, the strangeness of a muleback excursion through Nature's Wonderland to a gold mine, the bemusement of watching the Seven Dwarfs strolling casually through the crowd. In fact, the real magic of Disney's 'Magic Kingdom' is its atmosphere: an indefinable charm composed of an infinite number of harmonious details—and infinite pains constantly taken to keep it that way."

Of course, music is a very vital part of all the Disney parks. From the moment you walk into the park, you are surrounded by music. Each of the attractions and rides has its own music. There are marching bands and Dixieland jazz bands. There's a strolling Barbershop Quartet. There are musical parades. In addition to the music featured as a daily part of the park, a wide variety of special music functions and concerts are planned during the year, including sounds from rock through Dixieland jazz.

And the parks encourage young talent. Each year, representatives from college bands across the country are brought to Disneyland where they not only perform each day, but are given extensive instruction on various aspects of performing and the entertainment field. In the United States, through its parks, the Disney organization is the single largest employer of entertainers and musicians. Only the city of Las Vegas, with its numerous stage shows, exceeds Disney in the number of entertainers used.

Walt Disney envisioned the parks to be in a constant state of evolution. He did not foresee a static environment, but rather one in constant flux, reflecting the changing tastes of the American public and challenging the imaginations of his creative staff. As an example of this, in 1986 a major new attraction was opened, *Captain EO*, which is an exciting 3-D musical experience starring pop singer Michael Jackson.

At the end of the Fifties, the once-popular Western saw its demise, and in its place were bright, bouncy, happy films, many of which were comedies or musical pictures. Disney's first comedy release was *The Shaggy Dog*, which premiered in 1959 and starred Fred MacMurray. This led to a long Disney association for MacMurray, who would go on to star in a number of comedy features during the next decade.

Disney's first live-action musical film was *Babes in Toyland*, released in 1961. This Disney version of the Victor Herbert operetta starred Ray Bolger, Tommy Sands, and Annette Funicello, fresh from her success on the *Mickey Mouse Club* television show. George Bruns teamed with Mel Leven to turn out eleven original songs for the film, and the score was nominated for an Academy Award.

Many critics panned the film, but it did give the Disney staff an opportunity to experiment with an all-music picture, an experience which later paid off in *Mary Poppins*. Although *Babes In Toyland* received poor reviews, the music was applauded by the *New York Times* critic, who commented: "The librettos of most operettas are rudimentary at best. But the screenplay and the new lyrics by Mel Leven are current and have a jazz beat."

# CHAPTER TEN

## *The Sherman Years*

In 1960, Walt Disney took what was to become a most significant step musically. He brought into the studio the songwriting team of Richard M. and Robert B. Sherman— the Sherman Brothers. During the next eight years, they would write an incredible number of songs— some of which are among the most memorable Disney songs of all time. For Disney, this was the first time that he had a team of songwriters on his staff. Previously, he had used outside songwriters such as Sammy Fain or staff composers, with lyrics being written by virtually anyone at the studio. For example, in addition to writers such as Tom Blackburn and Mel Leven, Hazel George, who was the studio nurse, wrote the lyrics to a number of Disney songs under the pseudonym of "Gil" George.

*Opposite:* The famous Disney songwriting team of Richard M. (right) and, Robert B. Sherman.

How the Sherman Brothers arrived at Disney is a story reminiscent of how stars were reportedly discovered at the soda fountain in Schwab's drugstore in Hollywood. According to the Shermans, they had written a rock and roll song entitled "Tall Paul" to buck the trend at the time, which was for male vocalists to sing songs with female names in the title. The brothers had faith in the song and they had it recorded themselves and financed the production of 3,000 single records. They then painstakingly mailed each record to disc jockeys around the country. Like any good Hollywood-dream-come-true story, one day a representative from Disney's record company was visiting a disc jockey in New Jersey where he heard the record. He knew that the Disney record company was looking for an appropriate song to launch Annette Funicello as a popular singer. The rest is history.

"Tall Paul" went on to become a major hit for Annette. According to the Shermans, although *The Mickey Mouse Club* was off the air, Annette was still under contract to Disney, and the music publishing company was looking for material that she could record. Between 1958 and 1963, the Shermans wrote 36 songs for Annette, including the popular hits "Jo-Jo the Dog-Faced Boy" and "Pineapple Princess."

The Sherman Brothers' involvement with Walt Disney came about almost accidentally. As they describe it, they were building a reputation with Disney's music publishing company, but still had not actually met Walt. Disney, however, was aware of them because of their success with Annette. Jimmy Johnson, who headed music publishing at the time, asked them to write a song for a television film Annette was in, *The Horsemasters*. The Shermans wrote "Strummin' Song," and when they played it for Johnson, he took them to Walt's office to preview the song for him.

As Bob Sherman explains, "Walt absolutely floored us because, as soon as we walked in, he immediately began explaining in detail the story line for a completely different film. We didn't know what to say or do. Finally, when he had finished his lengthy explanation, we explained to Walt that we were there on another film. Well, he told us that since

we spent so much time listening to him, we should go ahead and see if we could come up with a title song for the picture. In the meantime, he told us that the 'Strummin' Song' would work for the TV show."

When the Shermans left Walt's office, they were somewhat disappointed that Walt was not more enthusiastic about the "Strummin' Song," since all he had said was "that'll work." Johnson explained that Walt was sparse with praise and so "that'll work" was indeed a high compliment.

At the time Walt gave them the new assignment, the title of the film was *We Belong Together*, a story about identical twins (both played by Hayley Mills) who were separated by divorced parents. The Shermans wrote a catchy rock and roll song for the film called "Let's Get Together," and Walt liked the song, but explained that the title of the film had been changed, so they'd need another title song. This time, the Shermans wrote "For Now, For Always," a lovely ballad for the estranged parents written in the style of a 1946 love song. Again, Walt liked the song but explained that the title of the film had been changed again. The Shermans went back to the drawing board and came up with a number called "Petticoats and Bluejeans," only to find out that the title of the film had changed once more. This song, however, was still used as an instrumental in the film, and its title was changed to "Whistlin' at the Boys." Finally, the Shermans wrote "The Parent Trap," which became the title of the 1961 film.

Their first song, "Let's Get Together," became a rock and roll hit recording and was a number one song in England. Hayley Mills performed the song in the movie and on the recording.

Bob Sherman recalled: "We were delighted to be working for Walt Disney. Our first impression of Hollywood when we arrived as youngsters in 1937 had been the street in front of the Carthay Circle Theatre resplendent with Disney characters for the premiere of *Snow White*. What a way to see Hollywood for the first time."

Among their next assignments was the title song for a Fred MacMurray film, *Bon Voyage* (1962), and through it they learned that Walt could have strong ideas about the type of songs he wanted in his pictures. For the title song, the Shermans wrote

# It's A Small World

*Theme From The Disneyland And
Walt Disney World Attraction*

Words and Music by
**RICHARD M. SHERMAN**
and
**ROBERT B. SHERMAN**

## WONDERLAND MUSIC CO., INC.

a lovely, sophisticated ballad that everyone working on the film thought was great. However, when they played the song for Walt, he didn't react. Instead he said, "What I'm looking for in this film is something upbeat, like 'California, Here I Come,' but in French." The Shermans went back to work, and the result was a bright, happy song that became the title song for the film.

For a film called *In Search of the Castaways* (1962), Disney wanted to cast Maurice Chevalier in the lead role, but knew Chevalier needed a strong song. So the Shermans wrote "Enjoy It," a lively song Chevalier sings while stranded in a tree, with the message that no matter what your circumstances are, enjoy it.

*In Search of the Castaways* also marked the thirty-year reunion for Chevalier and the Shermans' father, Al, who had written "Living in the Sunlight, Loving in the Moonlight" for Chevalier. The brothers wrote additional material for Chevalier while at Disney, including "Joie de Vivre," which was used in *Monkeys Go Home* (1967). When *The Aristocats* (1970) went into production, the Shermans were able to talk Chevalier out of retirement to record their title song. This was to be the final recording of his lengthy career.

Chevalier was a great fan of the Sherman Brothers' songs. Bob Sherman states, "He really enjoyed our music. In fact, for many years, he used 'It's A Small World' to open his stage show. And, he closed his show with 'There's a Great Big Beautiful Tomorrow,' which we wrote for the General Electric World's Fair exhibit." Following the World's Fair, that exhibit was moved to Disneyland where it was called GE's "Carousel of Progress." Then in 1973, the exhibit was relocated to Walt Disney World and the Shermans wrote a new song for it titled "The Best Time of Your Life."

Another song arising out of Disney's involvement with developing commercial exhibits for the World's Fair, and probably the Shermans' most famous song, was "It's a Small World." The song came about as a result of a serious problem Walt was having in coming up with appropriate music for a new exhibit. As Dick Sherman recalls: "One day Walt took us to where they built the *Audio-Animatronics* characters used at Disneyland and developed other special projects for Walt. He explained that they were building a Pepsi Cola-sponsored world's fair exhibit for UNICEF. The idea was to show the universality of man. He took us through a large mock-up which had mechanical dolls in native costumes from around the world, each singing their respective national songs. While the idea and animation were great, it was a cacophony of sound. Walt explained he wanted a simple song that could be sung in various languages and that would convey the message of human understanding."

This was a difficult assignment, as the lyrics had to be so simple that they did not become involved with complicated translations which would spoil the synchronization of the song throughout the entire exhibit. The result was:

*It's a world of laughter, a world of tears;*
*It's a world of hopes and a world of fears.*
*There's so much that we share*
*that it's time we're aware.*
*It's a small world after all.*

*There is just one moon and one golden sun*
*and a smile means friendship to ev'ry one,*
*Though the mountains divide*
*and the oceans are wide*
*It's a small world after all.*

*It's a small world after all*
*It's a small world after all*
*It's a small world after all*
*It's a small, small world.*

When the song had been written, the Shermans joined Disney at the mock-up and proceeded to demonstrate how the song would work with the different nationalities and how it would be synchronized between each country. As Dick Sherman recalls: "Walt seemed to like the song and felt that it would work. As we were driving back to the studio, Bob and I said we were thinking of waiving the royalties on the song since it was for a worthwhile cause. Well, Walt suddenly pulled the car over to the side of the road and said: 'Boys, that song is going to make you famous and put your children through college. Keep your royalties.' And, he was right. He had an incredible sense for what songs were going to make it, even though he had only heard a rough rendition sung by Bob and myself.''

''It's a Small World'' went on to become the most popular of any Disney song. It has been recorded more times and in more languages, has sold more records than any other Disney song, and has been used by virtually every major entertainer at one time or another. Today it is still heard daily at Disneyland, Walt Disney World, and Tokyo Disneyland.

Disney's first animated film in four years was *The Sword in the Stone* (1963), the story of young King Arthur and the magical sword, and the first time that the Shermans worked on an animated film. ''We enjoyed it immensely,'' said Bob Sherman, ''because with animated films the songs seem so much more important to the entire story line of the film. For example, the song 'Higitus Figitus' was written to both establish Merlin's rather bumbling character and to advance the story line of the film. That's something you don't get to do when just writing popular songs.''

The film was well received, but did not go on to be a box office smash. In the *New York Herald Tribune*, Judith Crist commented: ''The songs are bright and singable, the artwork lovely and the plot charming in its twists and turns.'' *Variety* said: ''The songs by Richard M. and Robert B. Sherman are in the familiar cartoon grove. They're agreeable tunes and go along nicely with the animated action.'' Again, the George Bruns score for the film was nominated for an Academy Award.

A particular favorite of the Shermans was *Winnie the Pooh*. As Dick Sherman recalled: ''In the beginning, we had a hard time truly understanding the significance of Milne's Pooh stories. One day during the filming of *Mary Poppins*, we asked Julie Andrews' husband, designer Tony Walton, about Pooh, since he was raised in England. He spent several hours with us enthusiastically explaining how important the Pooh stories were to him while he was growing up. When we were through, we finally had a feeling of how to understand the stories, how to get to the heart of them.''

Originally, *Winnie the Pooh* was planned as a full-length animated feature, but when Walt saw the finished storyboards, he decided against it. Dick Sherman recalled: ''Walt didn't feel the American public was ready for a feature-length film on the Pooh bear. Rather, he suggested a 26-minute featurette that would end with Pooh in the honey tree. He put the rest aside for future development. He was a visionary. When the first Pooh film was released in 1966, *Winnie the Pooh and the Honey Tree*, it was a modest success. But two years later, when the second featurette, *Winnie the Pooh and the Blustery Day* (1968), was issued, it was a smash hit, even winning an Oscar that year.''

A third featurette, *Winnie the Pooh and Tigger Too*, was released in 1974 and was also nominated for an Academy Award. In 1977, the three featurettes were combined into the full-length feature film that Walt had envisioned thirteen years previously, *The Many Adventures of Winnie the Pooh*.

Buddy Baker wrote the musical scores for the Pooh films. Of the songs written for Pooh, the Sherman Brothers' favorite is ''The Wonderful Thing about Tiggers.'' As Bob Sherman explained: ''This was really a fun song to write. It helped build the Tigger's character. What we enjoyed most was writing the last line: 'But, the most wonderful thing about Tiggers is I'm the only one.'''

During this period of time, Walt had become fascinated with English children's stories. *Winnie the Pooh* was an English tale, as was *Mary Poppins*. While he was negotiating the rights for P. L. Travers' Poppins stories, he acquired the rights to another English classic, *Bedknobs and Broomsticks* by Mary Norton, a story full of witchcraft and flying beds, and a natural for the Disney magical touch. As Bob Sherman recalled: ''Walt had the Mary Norton book before *Mary Poppins*. I remember that just before everything got going on *Poppins*, we were having problems getting approvals from P. L. Travers on the songs we had written. It was exasperating. One day Walt came to us and said, 'Don't worry boys, I've bought another story that deals with magic. If we can't work out things with Travers, we'll be able to use your stuff in the other picture.'''

Christopher Robin, Winnie the Pooh, and friends in
*The Many Adventures of Winnie the Pooh.*

*Bedknobs* was postponed until Disney had completed *Mary Poppins*. The film was finally produced and released in 1971 after Walt had died, and starred Angela Lansbury and David Tomlinson. One of the Shermans' songs for the film, "The Age of Not Believing," was nominated for a 1971 Academy Award, as was the musical score by the Shermans and Irwin Kostal, who had had a major success with the score and orchestration of *Mary Poppins*. Although *Bedknobs* did not come close to the fantastic success of *Mary Poppins*, it has been a very popular Disney film.

Another musical film that had the English touch was *The Happiest Millionaire* (1967), a Fred Mac-Murray comedy that featured British actor Tommy Steele. In the film, Fred MacMurray plays an eccentric millionaire who raises alligators. The story focuses on the bizarre nature of the household and the problems surrounding his daughter's engagement and wedding. The film introduced Lesley Ann Warren to the screen and co-starred Greer Garson and Geraldine Page. The film followed closely on the heels of *Mary Poppins* and was another full-scale musical production.

In recalling that film, Bob Sherman said: "The first song we wrote for the film was 'I'll Always Be Irish,' which Walt liked very much. There were many times, late in the afternoon, when Walt would ask us up to his office to play the song for him.

"Walt was interested in using Tommy Steele for the film, and asked us to go to New York with scriptwriter AJ Carothers to see him where he was appearing on Broadway in 'Half a Sixpence.' When we returned, we told Walt that Steele would be ideal for the part of the butler, but we felt he would need another big musical number to fully justify his talents for the picture. The result was 'Fortuosity,' which is a word we created, and which, as the opening number for Steele, helps establish his character." Again, Walt's philosophy was captured in the song about having faith in good fortune.

> *Well now, ain't this an elegant neighborhood;*
> *all the residents dress so fine.*
> *One day off the boat am I,*
> *with a job that's nearly mine.*
> *'Tis a job with an elegant millionaire,*
> *and his elegant family.*
> *Today I move from immigrant,*
> *to high society*
>
> Spoken: *You may call that luck,*
> *You may call it fortune,*
> *But me meself, I call it*
>
> *Fortuosity, That's me by word,*
> *Fortuosity, me twinkle in the eye word,*
> *Sometimes castles fall to the ground,*
> *but that's where four-leaf clovers are found.*
> *Fortuosity lucky chances,*
> *Fortuitious little, happy happenstances.*
> *I don't worry 'cause ev'rywhere I see*
> *that ev'ry bit of life is lit*
> *by Fortuosity!*
>
> *Fortuosity, That's me own word.*
> *Fortuosity, me never feel alone word.*
> *'Round a corner, under a tree,*
> *good fortune's waitin' just wait an' see.*
> *Fortuosity, lucky chances,*
> *Fortuitious little, happy happenstances,*
> *I keep smilin' 'cause my philosophy*
> *is, "Do your best and leave the rest to*
> *Fortuosity!'*

Tommy Steele

Another big number for Steele is a musical production of "Let's Have a Drink on It," with Steele and the rejected fiance, played by John Davidson, cavorting in an Irish pub.

For *The Jungle Book*, a full-length animated film released in 1967, the Shermans wrote all of the songs except "The Bare Necessities," which had been written earlier by Terry Gilkyson. The film was the last animated film that Walt was personally involved with before his death in 1966.

Based on the Mowgli books of Rudyard Kipling, *The Jungle Book* used the familiar voices of Phil Harris, Sebastian Cabot, Louis Prima, George Sanders, and a Disney favorite, Sterling Holloway. "The Bare Necessities" was sung by the gravel-voiced Phil Harris and was nominated for an Academy Award. Louis Prima, as the king of the monkeys in the film, did the freewheeling jazz vocal of "I Wan'na Be Like You."

For the close of the film, the Shermans wrote "My Own Home," a haunting song that conveys the feeling of the age-old siren song which lures boys from the sides of their mothers. In this case, the song explains Mowgli's decision to leave his jungle home to follow the lovely girl-child.

While they were at the studio, the Shermans wrote songs for twenty-seven feature films, in addition to songs for Disney television productions including "The Wonderful World of Color" theme song, Disneyland, and pop songs for the record company. Commenting on their experiences in working with Walt, they said: "Walt had a remarkable ability to visualize a completed film sequence from an artist's sketch or a writer's concept. He had the confidence to accept or reject ideas by his seat-of-the-pants instincts. He had an infallible memory for details. He could sense what a whole song would be from just a title or fragment of melody. Walt knew his people and their potentials better than they knew themselves."

*The Jungle Book* was the last animated film that Walt was personally involved with before his death in 1966.

# CHAPTER ELEVEN

## *The Ultimate Disney:* Mary Poppins

Walt Disney's greatest triumph was *Mary Poppins*, the pinnacle of a career dedicated to making people happy. It was a total synthesis of all that was Disney—animation, music, special effects, outstanding art, and superb casting and acting. The story is lovingly fashioned with the Disney touch, full of warmth and human understanding. Although subsequent Disney films would gross more in box-office receipts due to higher ticket prices, none came close to the magic and joy that Walt brought to the screen in *Mary Poppins*.

*Mary Poppins* was taken from a series of short stories by P.L. Travers. Walt was first introduced to the Poppins stories through his daughter, Diane, when she was a child. He fell in love with the stories and the idea of a nanny who could fly, and spent years trying to obtain the rights to the stories from Mrs. Travers, but to no avail, until after extensive work, he and his staff had developed a story outline and song score that satisfied her.

Before the Shermans had officially joined the Disney staff and were still writing songs "on spec" for the feature films, Walt gave them the Travers stories to review. What they had were a series of unrelated short stories that all featured Mary Poppins, a magical English nanny, as their central character.

The Shermans came back to Walt very excited about the possibilities in the stories. As Dick Sherman recalled: "We really fell in love with the stories. When we next met with Walt, we showed him the seven stories we selected as being our choices for the film. He reached over and got out his copy of the book, and we discovered we had picked the same seven chapters that Walt had already decided to use in the film."

Walt put the Shermans together with Don DaGradi, who had started in the art department at Disney and moved into screenwriting, and asked them to develop a screen treatment or outline and some songs. Dick Sherman explained: "From the beginning, we saw this in musical terms. We wanted to do a full-blown musical fantasy of the first magnitude. To achieve this, we set the story back in time to Edwardian London. We were able to convince Walt that this was the way to proceed. It also gave us the chance to write music and lyrics with English 'folk' and 'Music Hall' flavor."

Two of the songs that came out of these story outline sessions and were later used in the film were "Feed the Birds" and "Supercalifragilisticexpialidocious." Bob Sherman recalled: "In the Travers story of the old bird woman, she sat on the steps of St. Paul's Cathedral near the bank selling bags of bread crumbs and calling 'Feed the birds, tuppence a bag.' Well, to us it symbolized a wealth of human emotions—charity, love, human kindness, and compassion. We tried to get these feelings into the song":

*Early each day to the steps of Saint Paul's*
*The little old bird woman comes.*
*In her own special way to the people she calls,*
*"Come, buy my bags full of crumbs;*
*Come feed the little birds, show them you care*
*And you'll be glad if you do;*
*Their young ones are hungry, their nests are so bare;*
*All it takes is tuppence from you.*
*Feed the birds, tuppence a bag,*
*Tuppence, tuppence, tuppence a bag.*
*Feed the birds," that's what she cries,*
*While overhead, her birds fill the skies.*
*All around the cathedral the saints and apostles*
*Look down as she sells her wares.*
*Although you can't see it, you know they are smiling*
*Each time someone shows that he cares.*
*Though her words are simple and few,*
*Listen, listen, she's calling to you:*
*"Feed the birds, tuppence a bag,*
*Tuppence, tuppence, tuppence a bag."*

According to Bob Sherman, "I think this song was Walt's favorite. Many times, late on a Friday afternoon, he'd invite us into his office for a Scotch, simply to chat. Then he would get this look in his eye and turn to Dick and simply say, 'Play the song.' Years later he told us, 'This is the most beautiful song ever written for me.'"

"Supercalifragilisticexpialidocious" presented a different type of problem. Dick Sherman recalled: "When Mary Poppins takes the children through the chalk drawing from the world of reality into the world of fantasy, we wanted the children to have something to bring back with them, a talisman. In the

From Walt Disney's "MARY POPPINS"

# Supercalifragilisticexpialidocious

## Words and Music by RICHARD M. SHERMAN and ROBERT B. SHERMAN

**WALT DISNEY MUSIC COMPANY**
© Walt Disney Productions

**HAL LEONARD PUBLISHING CORPORATION**

book they bring back a starfish, but it turns to sand when they're back in the real world. As kids, we went to the Adirondacks for summer camp, and we recalled that one summer we had learned a word similar to 'Supercal.' It was a word that was longer than 'anti-disestablishmentarianism,' yet it gave us a word that no adult had. It was our special word and we wanted the Banks' children to have the same feeling.''

For two years, the "Poppins Project" was worked on by DaGradi and the Shermans, even though they were on other assignments. When Walt finally had a story outline and song score in which he was confident, he convinced Mrs. Travers that he would do justice to her stories, and he finally was able to obtain the rights to use them in a film. Bill Walsh, Disney's top writer/producer, was then assigned, with DaGradi, to create the screen play. The Shermans wrote 35 songs for the film, with 14 ultimately being used.

The next major hurdle for Walt was casting the role of Mary Poppins. He had considered several actresses, but Julie Andrews captivated him, especially her ability to whistle. She had starred for three and a half years in the Broadway smash hit *My Fair Lady*, and at the time, was creating a sensation on Broadway in *Camelot*.

When Walt approached her with the project, she was excited about playing the role. However, she was reluctant to commit herself to Disney, since Warner Brothers was planning a film version of *My Fair Lady* and she was hopeful of getting that role. As John Cottrell relates in his book, *The Unauthorized Life Story of a Super Star: Julie Andrews*: "In March 1962, however, the problem was solved for her. She was expecting a baby. . . . There was a possibility that Julie might play in *Camelot* on the London stage, but widespread expectation was that she would eventually make her film debut in the extravagant movie version of *My Fair Lady* now being planned by Jack L. Warner. No piece of casting was more obvious.''

But, reportedly under pressure from financial backers to use a proven box-office performer, Warner instead cast Audrey Hepburn in the title role of Eliza Doolittle. Julie promptly called Walt Disney and asked, "When do we start?"

As Cottrell noted: "She is the star who came to Hollywood as a nervous, unspoiled woman and who proceeded to win a best-actress Oscar at the first attempt.'' *Mary Poppins* launched Julie Andrews as a major film star. Her next film was *The Sound of Music*, which has also become a classic film. *Thoroughly Modern Millie*, her third film, broke all box-office records for Universal Studios. A few weeks before she received her Oscar for *Mary Poppins*, winning over Audrey Hepburn who wasn't even nominated for her role in *My Fair Lady*, Julie was presented the prestigious Golden Globe Award by the Hollywood Foreign Press Association. In accepting the award, Julie said, "Finally, I'd like to thank the man who made this possible—Jack Warner.''

Since *Mary Poppins* was being produced as a full-scale musical, the Shermans wanted someone who could bring the Broadway show sound to the screen. So Walt brought in Irwin Kostal, a well-known Broadway and television arranger who had recently won an Oscar for his co-scoring of *West Side Story*. Since the Shermans had worked closely with Don DaGradi on the story development, and with co-producer and co-scriptwriter Bill Walsh, the songs and music that the Shermans wrote literally flow through the film. Bob Sherman said, "Writing songs for *Mary Poppins* was a songwriter's dream. Each song we did had a purpose, a reason for being. Whether it is to build characterization or to carry the action, there is a purpose for each song.'' Leonard Maltin in *The Disney Films* commented: "Every song in the film suits its context perfectly and conveys emotions and ideas otherwise unexpressed in dialogue.''

The Walt Disney version of *Mary Poppins* opens with an uproar in the Banks household in London shortly after the turn of the century. The children's nanny has resigned; the children, Michael and Jane, played by Matthew Garber and Karen Dotrice, both of whom had previously appeared in Disney's *Three Lives of Thomasina*, are missing (actually they are trying to fly their kite in the park, and they damage it); and general confusion reigns. The next morning Mary Poppins arrives, dispatches the other aspiring nannies with a hurricane-force east wind, and calmly takes control of the Banks household.

"We needed a song early in the film," Dick Sherman explained, "that would establish a theme for Mary Poppins. At first we came up with a wistful ballad. But when Julie heard it, she asked that we do something with more bounce to it." The result was "A Spoonful of Sugar," which Julie sings as she uses her magical powers to help the children clean up their room. Throughout the film, Kostal uses the melody line of that song as a leitmotif in the background score whenever Mary is about to take center stage.

A song was also needed for Bert, played by the versatile Dick Van Dyke. The character of Bert combined several characters from the book—a one-man band, a sidewalk artist, and a chimney sweep. Dick Sherman recalled: "One day Bob came up with a line, 'One chimney, two chimney, three chimney sweep.' I left the room, the words running through my mind, when suddenly I had the melody line that went along with it. I rushed back into the room, played it on the piano, and 'Chim Chim Cher-ee' was born."

Irwin Kostal

*Chim chiminey, chim chiminey, chim chim cheree!*
*A sweep is as lucky, as lucky can be.*
*Chim, chiminey, chim chiminey, chim chim cheroo!*
*Good luck will rub off when I shakes 'ands with you.*
*Or blow me a kiss and that's lucky too.*
*Now, as the ladder of life 'as been strung,*
*You may think a sweep's on the bottom-most rung.*
*Though I spends me time in the ashes and smoke,*
*In this 'ole wide world there's no 'appier bloke.*

*Chim chiminey, chim chiminey, chim chim cheree!*
*A sweep is as lucky, as lucky can be.*
*Chim chiminey, chim chiminey, chim chim cheroo!*
*Good luck will rub off when I shakes 'ands with you.*
*Or blow me a kiss and that's lucky too.*
*I choose me bristles with pride, yes I do:*
*A broom for the shaft and a brush for the flue.*

*Up where the smoke is all billered and curled,*
*'Tween pavement and stars, is the chimney sweep world.*
*When there's 'ardly no day nor 'ardly no night,*
*There's things 'alf in shadow and 'alfway in light,*
*On the rooftops of London, coo, what a sight!*
*Chim chiminey, chim chiminey, chim chim cheree!*
*When you're with a sweep you're in glad company.*
*Nowhere is there a more 'appier crew*
*Than them wot sings "Chim chim cheree, chim cheroo!"*
*Chim chiminey, chim chim cheree, chim cheroo!*

The "Jolly Holiday" sequence is pure Disney musical fantasy, where Mary and Bert take the children through a chalk drawing on the sidewalk into a world of animated fantasy. In one scene, Bert joins four penguin waiters in a dance routine and then conducts a barnyard serenade in another scene. For the merry-go-round sequence, Kostal used glockenspiels to give the music a circus feel. When the horses come alive and peel off to join a fox hunt, Kostal uses nine French horns to convey the feeling of the hunt. Next, in a horse race, the foursome rejoin and when Mary wins, she tells everyone that she thought it was "Supercalifragilisticexpialidocious." Rain begins to fall and washes away the chalk drawing, and the children find themselves back on the streets of London.

When the children return home, they are too excited to go to sleep, so Mary uses reverse psychology with a beautiful ballad/lullaby "Stay Awake." For the soundtrack, Kostal used a unique combination of six cellos and six violas to give the song a warm, loving feeling. When a poll was conducted at the studio before the release of the film, this song was voted the favorite.

The children's adventures continue the next day when they visit Mary's uncle Albert, played by Ed Wynn, who has a serious case of excessive laughter. The infectious "I Love to Laugh" soon has the children floating around the room and bouncing off the ceiling.

When the children return home, their father (played by David Tomlinson) lectures on his desire for orderliness and proper decorum in the song "A British Bank." Mary encourages him to take the children to the bank where he works. That night she tells Michael and Jane about the old bird woman by singing "Feed the Birds."

On their way to the bank, the children want to spend their tuppence to feed the birds, but they are ushered into the bank instead. When the elderly chairman, also played by Dick Van Dyke, tries to deposit their tuppence with the song "Fidelity Fiduciary Bank," the children's outraged cry for their money causes a run on the bank.

The children flee, meet up with Bert, and later with Mary. Bert is in his chimney-sweep clothes, and everyone joins him in the song, "Chim Chim Cher-ee." A little later, they join Bert on the rooftops with his chimney-sweep pals for a rollicking dance number, "Step In Time," which ends up in the Banks' living room, soot and all.

How the song "Step In Time" came to be was explained by Bob Sherman: "One afternoon we received a call to come over to Walt's office right away. When we arrived, we encountered an incredible sight. There was Walt, matte artist Peter Ellenshaw, and scriptwriters Don DaGradi and Bill Walsh, all prancing in a circle around the room, kicking their knees high. Pencils were flying out of their pockets as they sang a bawdy, old Cockney pub song 'Knees Up Mother Brown.' Walt shouted to us, 'This's what we need for the rooftop dance.' In all honesty, our 'Step In Time' is something like it, but a lot more Disney."

At this point in the story, Mr. Banks is summoned to the bank, and on the way, decides his children are more important to him than the bank. He resigns in a hilarious scene complete with his being stripped of his umbrella and bowler hat. Upon his return home, he disappears into the basement and emerges with his children's kite repaired. As a kite is used in the opening of the film, it also closes it, and the final song is "Let's Go Fly a Kite."

With the children happily reunited with their parents, Mary raises her umbrella and is whisked away by the west wind—her mission complete.

*Mary Poppins* received an incredible thirteen Academy Award nominations and won Oscars in five categories. Besides Julie Andrews' Oscar for best actress, the first time for a Disney star, the Shermans received two Oscars—one for the song "Chim Chim Cher-ee" and the other for original musical score. Irwin Kostal was nominated for best adaptation of an original score, and the film received other Oscars for film editing and special effects.

*Mary Poppins* was the one Disney film that received unanimous accolades from the critics. In the *New York Times*, Bosley Crowther commented: "... *praise heaven there are such as they [Disney] still making films.*" Hollis Alpert in *The Saturday Review* called it "a burst of sheer frolicsome delight, one of the most magnificent pieces of entertainment to come from Hollywood." *Variety* said, "All the magic that audiences have come to associate with Disney films down through the years comes to life with eloquent and delicious lustre in this musical fantasy."

# CHAPTER TWELVE
## *The Disney Legacy*

**A**lthough Walt Disney died in December 1966, the spirit he instilled at the studio lives on. In the twenty years following his death, the studio has maintained the highest quality of film production in the Disney tradition. No other studio has since come close to the quality or overall output of animated films.

Many of the films that were released in the immediate years following Walt's death were films that he had been personally involved with. When he died, his staff had stacks of ideas and story outlines for future projects, and during the next ten years, many of these were brought to reality, including his dream of EPCOT— the Experimental Prototype Community of Tomorrow— at Walt Disney World.

But most importantly, Walt left a part of himself behind with each individual that he came in contact with at the studio, and he left the Disney magic touch in good hands. The Sherman Brothers explained that they still receive letters addressed to the studio complimenting them on film musicals they've worked on since Walt's death that were not Disney productions, among them *Chitty Chitty Bang Bang*, *Charlotte's Web*, *The Slipper and the Rose*, and *Tom Sawyer*. Dick Sherman said: "The people don't realize that none of these films were Disney productions. Walt had nothing to do with any of them. . . or did he?"

In the years following Walt's death, several films were produced that are particularly noteworthy for their music, such as *The One and Only, Genuine, Original Family Band* (1968). This film, which was originally planned as a two-part television show titled "The Family Band," was based on the book *Nebraska 1888* by Laura Bowers Van Nuys about her family's band that performed at the 1888 Democratic convention. Walt had asked the Shermans to give him some help on it because he felt it was too flat, and the Shermans came up with the title song, which was then used as the title for the picture. After hearing the song, Walt decided to add more songs to the picture and turn it into a musical. In all, the Shermans wrote eleven songs for the film.

The animated feature *The Aristocats* (1970) featured cats as the stars, and Thomas O'Malley as the film's favorite. This film re-established the pre-eminence of the Disney studio in animation. The musical score for the film was written by George Bruns, with songs written by the Sherman Brothers, Terry Gilkyson, Floyd Huddleston, and Al Rinker. As *Time* commented: "But for the integration of music, comedy and plot, *The Aristocats* has no rivals."

The next animated feature, *Robin Hood*, was released in 1973. This version of the classic tale was

*The Aristocats.*

*The Rescuers.*

made again using animals as the characters, for example, Robin and Maid Marian are depicted as foxes. And again, the studio used familiar voices for the characters including Phil Harris, Andy Devine, Peter Ustinov, and Pat Buttram.

Ken Anderson, who was responsible for developing the story concept, recalled: "Camera schedules were set up, and George Bruns, the musical director, began outlining the score and special songs which were needed. Johnny Mercer wrote new lyrics for 'The Phony King of England.' Roger Miller, who is the vocal talent for Allen-a-dale, the minstrel rooster, wrote and recorded 'Oo-de-Lally,' a song based on one of Robin's favorite sayings; 'Whistle Stop,' a kind of nonsense hum-along, whistling tune; and 'Not in Nottingham,' a ballad describing the plight of the overtaxed peasants.

Bruns himself wrote the music and Floyd Huddleston the lyrics for 'Love,' Maid Marian's pretty message to Robin." "Love" was nominated for an Academy Award.

1977 resulted in a banner year for Disney music, with two songs nominated for Academy Awards—"Someone's Waiting for You" from *The Rescuers* and "Candle on the Water" from *Pete's Dragon.*

*The Rescuers* was produced as a fully animated feature for a staggering cost of $7 million, yet it grossed more than any previous Disney film. The film follows the adventures of two mice (with the voices of Bob Newhart and Eva Gabor) who are representatives of an international mouse organization, the Rescue Aid Society, as they set out to rescue a kidnaped orphan.

Sammy Fain (left) wrote the music for the Oscar-nominated song "Someone's Waiting For You" from *The Rescuers*, and Artie Butler wrote the film score.

Carol Connors (right) and Ayn Robbins wrote the songs for *The Rescuers*.

Frank Thomas and Ollie Johnston, who were animation directors on the film, in their book *Disney Animation*, recalled how the film's score contributed to the mouse characters, Bernard and Bianca: "We had worked hard on *The Rescuers* trying to make the mice seem very small and inadequate to the task facing them, but the confidence and spirit in the voices seemed to dispel any concern we could develop for them. When Artie Butler wrote the music, he felt the predicament of the mice acutely and wrote music that immediately made their task enormous, while somehow keeping them virtually helpless. When they tried to move the huge diamond from its hiding place, the score added a good one hundred pounds to the weight of the gem. The animator exclaimed, 'I tried to make the mice strain and heave and use every bit of their strength when they pushed against the diamond, but this—this exhausts me!'"

The songs for the film, written by Carol Connors and Ayn Robbins, deliver an overall message of hope. In "Tomorrow Is Another Day," the mice express hope of a successful search, and in the Oscar-nominated "Someone's Waiting for You," the young orphan expresses hope that she will belong to someone someday. Disney veteran, Sammy Fain, provided the music for this song.

*Pete's Dragon* was released later in 1977 and was a musical fantasy complete with animation in the tradition of *Mary Poppins*. This film was based on a thirteen-page synopsis that Walt had prepared before his death, and its success firmly established that the studio could still recapture the Disney magic.

The star and lead vocalist of *Pete's Dragon* was major pop singer Helen Reddy, backed by an outstanding cast including such seasoned performers as Mickey Rooney, Jim Dale, Red Buttons, Shelley Winters, and as the voice of Elliott the dragon, Charlie Callas.

The song score for the film was done by Al Kasha and Joel Hirschhorn, both of whom had earned Oscars for their "Morning After" from *The*

Irwin Kostal (right) arranged and conducted the music for *Pete's Dragon,* and Al Kasha (center) and Joel Hirschhorn (left) wrote the songs. All three were nominated for Academy Awards.

*Poseidon Adventure* and "We May Never Love Like This Again" from *The Towering Inferno.* Irwin Kostal was selected to handle the arranging and conducting, and was once again nominated for an Academy Award for his brilliant scoring. Kasha and Hirschhorn also shared in that honor.

Probably the most memorable song from this film is performed by Helen Reddy during one of the film's most touching scenes. As she is atop the lighthouse, wistfully looking out to sea for her lost love, Reddy tells her love she is his "Candle on the Water." Kasha explained: "This is a step-out song. That is, Helen steps out of the action, goes up to the lighthouse, and it gives her an opportunity in the film to fully utilize her talent for singing a ballad."

A truly delightful song, "It's Not Easy," provides Pete with an opportunity to describe his friendship with Elliot. Kasha and Hirschhorn wrote this song with the intention that it would be a "charm"

song. "It has warmth and honesty. We wanted to get the audience emotionally involved."

Other song highlights from *Pete's Dragon* included "Brazzle Dazzle Day," a bright, bouncy number sung by Reddy, and "I Saw a Dragon," a comical sequence that turns into a major dance number featuring Mickey Rooney. All in all, *Pete's Dragon* was another example of the rich music and musical talent that abound in Disney films.

In the summer of 1982, Disney released *Tron,* fully demonstrating that the studio was capable of advancing the state of the art of motion picture production—of going beyond what everyone else was doing, and taking the type of creative risks that Walt had taken to prove his ideas would work.

*Tron* was an experiment in computerized visuals and sound, and it was the first film to utilize completely computer-generated animation for its visuals, effectively combining this type of animation with live-action to portray the video-game world of Tron and the fantastic adventures that occur within it. Equally unique was the music and sound, which married synthesized sound to real acoustical sound, brilliantly projecting the feeling of this strange world in the film. Wendy Carlos was selected to compose the score and handle the orchestrations. Carlos first achieved notice with the release of her *Switched-on Bach* recordings in 1968 where she adapted this classical material for a synthesizer that she and Robert Moog had developed.

In a lengthy interview in *CinemaScore*, Carlos described the role of the synthesizer and how it was used for *Tron*: "In most orchestral music, you usually have a great interplay of the instruments. Well-orchestrated music has notes coming from all the sections rapidly falling one after another; it gives a marvelous texture and a nice color. I would think that an imaginative composer could make a synthesizer go along as being a color that is in there underneath every so often, and occasionally let it rise to the surface for a momentary solo, the way you do with woodwinds or what-have-you. . . it's (synthesizer) likely to be one of the most useful members of the orchestra for film scoring just because it embraces so many things that can fall into almost a pseudo-concrete kind of style that suggest dramatic events far more easily than you can do with traditional instruments. It's like a chorus;. . . .

"I'd been looking for a chance to incorporate orchestra with synthesizer in some way so that the synthesizer was really an equal part of the orchestra in the full sense, not the way it's usually used, just for a few solo lines. . . . I'm going to try and produce a score that has some areas that are heavy on the electronics and other areas which are heavy on the orchestra, but which, by and large, will blend the two most of the time and make the boundaries unclear, so that the audience should be as unconcerned with whether they're hearing synthesizer or live instruments as they are with whether they're watching a live photograph or a computer-generated one. The result is that I've written a score for a large orchestra—we used the London Philharmonic and employed a hundred and five pieces on it. . . . I'm synching to their performances.

". . . that score was recorded with the instruments separated as much as we could do in the large hall where we recorded it. That gave me a mix which allowed the solo woodwinds, or whatever, to be put down a bit low, and have synthesizers supplement in on top of them, and in such a timbre that the result is that the ear probably doesn't recognize that there's another instrument underneath it. . . . making synthesizers do things that, in the past, have sounded quite like being an orchestra, and that tends to make them seem fairly diffuse, fairly hard to pick out."

The animation, story and music for *Tron* were a powerful combination, but the film enjoyed only moderate success at the box office. As Leonard Maltin notes in *The Disney Films*: "For the first time since anyone can remember, the studio was actually riding the crest of a wave, capitalizing on a trend as it was peaking—not after it had faded. . . . the ingredients of *Tron* turned out to be more impressive than the film itself. And while it was far from a flop at the box office, its failure to become a blockbuster of the George Lucas/Steven Spielberg variety made it seem that way."

Wendy Carlos
(Photo by Vernon Smith)

# A TRIBUTE

In the more than fifty years since Disney's first song, "Minnie's Yoo-Hoo," was written, Disney and his staff of musical wizards made immense contributions to music and films. The techniques they developed and perfected to intricately blend film and music are still being used today. Most importantly, however, they demonstrated how music could become an integral part of film. They approached music in a way in which no one had approached it before, with a keen appreciation for the important role music could have in a film, and they put music on a new level for all film makers who followed them.

The early composers and arrangers at Disney — Carl Stalling, Frank Churchill, Paul Smith, and Leigh Harline — all had a major impact on how music is used in films today. They were the visionaries that Walt inspired to achieve new heights in music, and although none of them became household names, their songs and music certainly did, establishing for them their proper place in music history.

The many who followed these Disney pioneers have continued to build on that foundation. The music and songs from Disney were uplifting, giving the audience the continuing hope that dreams really do come true. The Disney composers and lyricists did not write a song for the sake of the song, but rather as an integral part of the film. The fact that many of their songs became popular hits was an add-ed, and many times unexpected, bonus. And behind each song is found Walt Disney, who had the gift of inspiring people to give their very best.

"Genius" is the only word that can describe Walt Disney's contributions to our culture. Worldwide, he is acclaimed for the films that he brought to life. Over the years, he has captured the hearts of millions; he has given countless people hope; and during periods of turmoil in our history, he has given us brief moments of respite. Most importantly, however, he has thoroughly *entertained* us.

As one close associate of Disney's noted, his films had heart. And so did his music. His songs reached our innermost selves with messages of love, hope, and human compassion — messages that will live for years to come. Walt truly believed in these messages, and because of his strong faith in the goodness that life can hold for all of us, generations to come will be reminded of these hopes and dreams as they've been so purely expressed by Jiminy Cricket:

*When you wish upon a star*
*Makes no diff'rence who you are*
*Anything your heart desires will come to you.*
*. . . When you wish upon a star*
*Your dreams come true.*

# INDEX

# INDEX OF PHOTOGRAPHS